Second Chance to Meraki

Most of us don't get it right the first time and not many get the choice of a second chance. So, if a 'second chance' knocks at your door, don't give a second thought - embrace it with all your being.

Kettaki

ISBN 978-93-5610-676-5

Published in India 2022 by Pencil

A brand of
One Point Six Technologies Pvt. Ltd.
123, Building J2, Shram Seva Premises,
Wadala Truck Terminal, Wadala (E)
Mumbai 400037, Maharashtra, INDIA
E connect@thepencilapp.com
W www.thepencilapp.com

Dedication

To everyone who believes - what you seek is seeking you.

About the author

Hey Reader ☺

We have something in common. That's the reason why you are holding this book. Well, what exactly we have in common I leave it for you to discover through these pages.

Apart from that, you will find me living in the city that never sleeps, shuffling between writing stories and freelancing, aspiring to be a screenwriter someday soon and having a secret affair with the Moon.

So, ya, that's about me for now, *leaving a piece of me in my work*, which is also the meaning of the word *Meraki.*

Happy reading all the Meraki Conversations I have compiled for You.
You can reach out to me on my IG handle @themerakiwoman

CONTENTS

Second Chance to Meraki

Meraki is what happens to you, when you leave a piece of your soul in anything and everything that you love to do.

I have juggled this very question all my life - whether you choose or whether you are chosen. I know what I want to do but I don't know what I want to do. I know I want to do something soul-involving, but I don't know where exactly to involve my soul.

I seem to like a lot of things, so I don't know what to choose or should I just wait for something to choose me and keep trying out things till then.
I am already in my thirties and it pains me to say that ever since I have understood the concept of *ikigai*, it has made me 'feel lost' more than I was. Because, back then, I didn't have a means to find out things about myself or the thing that I would dedicate myself to, but today, when I have the means, I am still there, trying out things.

And, that's when I conceived this idea of **Second Chance to Meraki.** I have found some peace with the acceptance that **there's a reason Life believes in 2nd chances because most people don't get it right the first time.**

By most, I mean, most of this generation, the Gen Y where I belong and the Gen Z who are sort of tomorrow's future. What we have in abundance are choices and it's a good thing but do we know how to use this 'freedom to choose' to build a *meraki* way of life?

Prelude

2020 was my moment of truth for many reasons - personal and professional. And I am certain that it was a year of revelation for many people.

There are **two types of struggles** for a human (other than the survival ones) - **fighting with yourself** and trying to be what you are not for the sake of others and **fighting for yourself** for the sake of protecting what you are. But before being able to do that, **one must also know who you are!**

Getting in touch with your authentic self is the key here because it's very easy to get influenced – partly because of the digital age we live in and partly by the societal conditioning we are groomed into.

I am not here to tell you so and so is hard or easy. Because, nothing is easy. I am here to tell you, **you can and you must choose your hard**, before life puts you somewhere, where the hard isn't what you chose.

Life will be hard as a painter or a doctor. But, if you want to paint, the hard will be worth something and you may save a life, if not, lives! That one life, your life, may save other lost lives like yours. That one life, a relatively happier life, your life, can spread happiness and maybe someday, **one life at a time, the world could be a happier place.**

Is there a bigger happiness than getting to do what you love to do? Don't choose the pain of having to become a doctor when you can choose the pain that comes with painting.

No-pain is never an option, so if you are going to go through it anyway, make it worthy. With the advent of 2020 and a lot of time for self-introspection, something hit me super hard. I had been 'running away' from something all my life.

That always made me super restless because I didn't know what I was running away from. I figured I was running away from myself, from being me, from being my own version. It's not always necessary that 'our version of oneself' is accepted by everyone around us, even our loved ones. But it's crucial one accepts it for oneself - good, bad, ugly - one can't disown a part of oneself.

When you keep disowning, running away, it grows bigger and bigger like a shadow chasing you and you can't get rid of it because it's very much a part of you. It becomes a life pattern sooner than you know and keeps affecting every decision you make.

I had my 'now or never' moment, the day of my birthday in 2020. Every year few days before my birthday, I have a phase, a really dark one wherein I cry myself to bed, accusing myself of having a purposeless life, a good life if you look at it, but always leaving me questioning, *"Am I doing my bit to keep this earn, these blessings?"*

I mean, imagine being broken so much that I had a hard time even accepting the good things life has blessed me with. This is the level of damage that happens to your self-esteem when you keep running away from yourself and imagine making decisions from this state of mind! In my quest of finding meaning to life, I have tried my hand at a lot of things only to realize - what you want may not always be what you need in the real long run of life. I have gone from believing something to completely disbelieving that same thing and vice versa.

Here's a quick disclaimer: This book may not be for everyone at the onset. It's for those who identify themselves with an eerie kind of restless energy, a little towards being a misfit, but seeking really bad to find their *meraki way of life* and allowing themselves that second chance.

In my state of brokenness, I had reached a level of self-hatred that denied me the courage to be kind to myself, to give myself the chance to stop running away, to start facing, to start admitting, to start accepting, to start changing.

But something changed, maybe I chose to change, maybe it was my time to be chosen – whatever be the case, I found the courage, to find my way back to being me and I want to pass this ***meraki-baton*** to you in the hope that you will pass it on to whoever is seeking it.

Maybe this is how one chooses to be chosen

Happy Reading, Meraki Reading!

Before you begin reading, set your intention with the book.

Ask yourself this…

What will you do if you are given a second chance?

Every chapter of this book has a blank page for you to take notes; I feel that helps while reading a book, because that's usually how I read a book!

~ ~ MY MERAKI NOTES ~ ~

Meraki Conversations

1. Lifeline, not deadline…

2. Happyholic or workaholic?

3. Get fascinated with yourself!

4. Balance the Effort with Surrender.

5. Marry the Moment :D

6. Labels or Experiences?

7. Lost and Found !

8. Are you in a relationship with yourself?

1. Lifeline; not deadline.

I feel I have been trying to write this book since forever but haven't found the right time to get it right! And when I say, right time, all I mean is, checking off some boxes, like ...

Who am I, really, that people will pick this book? I haven't accomplished as much that will put me on pedestal for others to choose this book, just because I have written it.

To write a self-help book, don't you have to help yourself first? I mean, obviously, right? I should have it all figured out, if I claim to 'self-help' other people. But I don't have it all figured out.

I only have that much figured, right now, that I know, will lead to the next step of figuring out.

This realization, rather this sense of self-awareness that has come to me (I have paid quite a price for it, hasn't really come to me easy) gives me the courage to take this up at a state when I am still a work-in-progress project myself. But yes, progress is the important word here.

And Life has taught me quite recently that, that much is enough (most of the times); life reveals to you only how much you can handle. It might be hard to agree to this, but try and give this a thought. **Life knows a lot more than you do** what will make you, what will break you! That's why it always throws different kinds of challenges to different people. Trusting how much you know 'in the moment' is more important than anything else; because no one has it all figured out.

The bigger forces know what can break you totally vs what can break you just enough to push you to be better.

~s~c~m~

Life has a better understanding of things and most often the Universe gives you things that you can deal in the moment. Most often we think/feel we want something; but what we need is what the Universe serves us.

Sometimes, knowing too much at the wrong time can do more harm than help. So, it's important we trust that the Universe knows better and will serve us and help us with the right things and right time. And, most importantly; something to always keep in mind as you proceed reading this is; that **everyone's timeline is different.**

We shouldn't be chasing deadlines, when **what we actually are is a timeline**. There are countless examples of people who began late, but are doing better than most who started early; who aced in school but couldn't fare in real life, who were average beings in college but are experts in their segment today. Doesn't mean that one must procrastinate and start late on purpose; it only means one mustn't beat oneself up for starting late.

The day you realize, what is it you want to do in life, be in life, is the day you can mark as the start-point of the measure scale.

Don't compare yourself with others, when you can measure your progress with yourself. Since recently, I have stopped dwelling on questions like, why am I a late-bloomer, what I could have done or what I could have avoided doing had I understood certain things earlier in life.

If it flows, it stays; if it is forced it breaks. I was so fixated about why so-and-so wasn't the way I wanted it, or why I wasn't living up to my own expectation that all my energy used to get exhausted on what happened in the past vs what I want to do in the NOW.

But I realized that,
you start glowing differently, when you know, when you affirm to yourself that, you are exactly where you need to be; not early, not late, on time!

With all the good and bad experiences I have had in life, one thing I have learnt is - **I will be guided, all I have to do, is be.**

Be kind, not weak.

Be genuine, not a fool.

Be honest, but don't hurt anyone.

Be yourself, seek your own validation.

Allow the FORCES to help you, be you, to help you be what you are meant to be.

This is what gives me the courage, faith and confidence to take this up, to take this up at a stage, where I am probably not in the Jay Shetty leagues, but this still is my journey and I would want to document my journey as much as I would want to celebrate the destination.

Because, **journey is something you will spend more time with, while destination is like a stop, it will come and go.**

There's this amazing dialogue from one of my favorite Bollywood movies, *"Simple hai, kuch logon ke sath sirf waqt bitane se sab kuch sahi ho jata hai."*

And by *'kuch log'* I mean, that one person with whom you spend most of your time with – **yourself**.

Spend some time alone, believe me, it is sassy AF, it's legit self-discovery.

What once started as a drunk-session with friends, gave me an answer I was looking for, for years. And as the answer came to me, I realized that there couldn't have been a better timing for it.

I felt I was led to the answer because of the strong seeking.

The question was very simple - Who am I?

Who am I?
Kettaki.

Who is Kettaki?
Marketing professional
Aspiring Ted Ex Speaker

These are the kind of answers we usually have; when asked *'who are you'* we often associate it with *'what we do'* which in reality is just a part of who we are. So, probe yourself more.

When you are not being a marketing professional, who are you? I am someone's daughter, someone's partner, someone's sister, someone's inspiration, someone's colleague, someone's teacher, I am also a writer, I am also a dreamer, I am hope, I am Life, I am Meraki.

I am a story. We all are.

And we get to choose who to be in our story.

Who am I?
I am whatever I chose to be :)

You can become anything you want only as long as you are living your full potential and there is no half in and half out - there shouldn't be.

Life is about living and in living
we find our becoming.

You will be led to the right things at the right time. Right for you, may not be right for someone else. For you at a given point, the right thing could be getting fired from your job because that's how maybe you are forced to look for another job which is probably far better than the previous one or this is precisely how you take that long awaited plunge to start that business you always wanted to start or take that solo trip or anything for that matter.

Allow LIFE to lead you where you are
supposed to be led, to push you into
becoming what you are meant to be.

~s~c~m~

I have also come to believe that, Universe will teach you what you need to learn in this journey as a Soul, only when you are *'ready to learn'* but if you keep running away from that, **that what is meant to be your learning as a human soul**, Life will keep throwing in your face, the same experiences, over and over again, until you learn. **This is what we also call patterns.**

Are you someone who keeps attracting a certain type of people in your life and then end up cursing yourself for attracting the same type of people, who give you a similar kind of hurt and every time you tell yourself - No - I won't repeat this again with the next person - but somehow, it's the same!

Same goes for similar kind of experiences, maybe something as serious as missing out on an admission by a few marks to something that happens on a daily basis like missing your usual train although you were on time today, because the train came by a little early.

If you are smiling at this, in your head, you know exactly what I mean and the take away from this smile (this silent, crooked, half-hearted, calling yourself an idiot-*wala*-smile) is that you are not learning what the Universe is trying to teach you.

**You got to sit back and identify what exactly that is;
what exactly you are running away from;
in search of that something.**

What exactly is your language when you are talking to yourself when you missed that admission or that train? How exactly is that person treating me when something doesn't happen as per his/her will? Ask yourself these questions.
When we meet someone and we have this feeling that something has clicked - it's most often your own void that you are looking to fill up, it's most often the emptiness of something or the excess of something inside of you, that is looking for a way out.

The reason I am mentioning this here is that, you are the average of five people you spend the most time with.

Who we meet depends on who we attract at an energy level, **who we attract at an energy level depends very much on the relationship you have with yourself,** the patterns in your subconscious formed due to years of societal conditioning, early stages of upbringing and your dialogue with yourself that constantly determines your every action.

Thus, people comprise a huge part in your making and breaking and hence it is impertinent that you make yourself whole as an individual – accept both, your weakness and strength – gracefully.

Love yourself in entirety –
don't run away from your flaws,
don't deny your failures, don't reject your fears.

Embrace it all as you.

Once you do, you will emerge as a better person, as a humble person, as an understanding person, as an empathetic person, as a grateful person. And when you have these by your side, everything seems effortless, goals become mere habits, success and failures become mere learnings, **happiness and joy become your very nature, you flow.**

Trust me, I don't mean to sound preachy, I hope I am not!!!

I say all this from my experience and all I want to do is share with you all. The sooner you realize this, the sooner you can channelize it, channelize inward, be a better person, be whatever you want to be!

But, let me tell you one more thing, the journey
towards self-discovery sucks,
it's a fight every day!

Because you meet parts of yourself that
you never thought were you.

You meet parts of you that you have shunned away thinking it's not you, thinking it can't be you, because you have been taught through ages of generational trauma and upbringing about what is socially-right, what is socially-wrong.

It's a battle everyday because you have to give yourself that pep-talk everyday.

These are the parts inside you, that you go about finding in others, for validation, thus always attracting a 'certain type of people'. The moment you start accepting those rejected parts of your own self, embrace the way you are, I am not even talking about right or wrong, j**ust unconditionally accepting the very nature of you, is the moment you start healing.**

This marks the beginning of the most beautiful journey – finding your authentic self.

Now, you start attracting a whole lot of different people. Who are your tribe, you give you a sense of anchoring and belonging!

Let me remind you again that, the inner-work is even more difficult, even more challenging, even more gruesome, but at the other end of that inner-work-path, is a brand new you :)

Just to give an example, there is a part of you who yearns to dance but it been taught to you that it's not what decent people do; there is a part of you who yearns to paint but you have been told that it is not something that pays bills, there is a part of you who yearns to be a teacher, but you belong to a family of doctors and lawyers, there is a part of you who prefers to be a dog-mother more than anything else but societal conditions make you choose differently.

There could be millions of such scenarios – small and big – that we struggle through, live by, every day. **My question is, why just live by?** No one can skip struggle, but you must get to choose your struggle – **make a choice to struggle in the area of life that gives you fulfillment.**

~s~c~m~

I am sure, you have heard this before; life is so often about the choices we make, the chances we take; I just want to add one more dimension to this - **life is also about the choices we don't make, the chances we don't take** the choices, we know deep within that we should make, we unknowingly, unwillingly let go, because we are too busy say Yes to things we should say No to.

How can there be space for things you want to do, when your hands are full of things you don't want to do, full of things you don't really care about as much as the things you haven't said a Yes to.

Being able to say No is a power most of us underestimate. I once belonged to that party too. **What you say No will determine what you will say a Yes to.** Don't ditch the chances, we know deep within that are meant for us, waiting, to be chosen by us because you are being a Yes-man or a Yes-woman.

There are always two types of people - ones who aren't aware of what is what, of what possibilities could do, if they give it a shot and the ones who are on the edge, who are aware of what possibilities could do and yet, they chose to stay ordinary, to not take that plunge - because of fear of falling in unknown territories, because of fear of being an outcast. Staying safe and stagnant or staying unsettled and open to possibilities - what do you choose?

Why *second chance to meraki?* Why this name?

**It's because if you are seeking, really seeking something,
life does give you a second chance,
because life wants to see you,
be you, be your truest fullest potential.**

Well, what I have said sounds very neat and structured, maybe wise and all super! But I have had a hard time arriving here, with this word craft, with this structure.

And that's why I felt very strongly that I need to share this with people like me, who are in the same boat as I was, so that there's one question less that haunts them *'pehle kyu nahi realize kiya'.'* Why didn't I realize/understand/know this earlier in life?

I have spent a lot of my time and energy comparing myself with others - my flaws vs their forte, my shortcoming vs their success - and in doing this, I have often undermined the progress I made because my scale of comparison was never me - I have always considered myself *'not good enough'* because it has always been *'me vs everyone else'* instead of being *'me vs me'*.'

And for this reason, I have always been an unhappy person, despite having so much more than most others. I was never an ungrateful person, but at the same time, I wasn't appreciative as much as I should have been for all the blessings because I always kept telling myself '*I wasn't good enough, if I am not good enough, I can't receive all these blessings'*

I was taking effort but things were not manifesting the way I wanted to because I realized this later that, even in the effort I took, I was always self-doubting, I wasn't really balancing it with surrender and belief.

The more you are aligned with this sense of anchoring, the more you will be able to balance 'the effort and the surrender'. I will be writing more about this balance, in the subsequent chapters. **But the takeaway so far is 'trust the timing of your life', because this life is not a deadline, it's a lifeline.**

Last but not the least...
If you identify yourself with an eerie kind of restless energy, a little towards, *'not really fitting in'*, a little towards, *'being a rebel about human nature, but pro-nature'*, a little towards, *'carrying within a fleeting feeling that no words can describe'*, a little towards, *'seeking a weird sort of happiness in disruption'* a little towards, *'feeling triumph when nature shows man its place for messing with it'* but only to realize how it all fit

and was meant to be and couldn't have been any other way - had it been any other way, it just wouldn't have made any sense.

Only if you relate, plunge in, deeper into the pages of this book. Until then, stay at the shores, till this book is acclaimed by the who's who - which might make you pick this up again. That's because we belong to that majority of humanity who will appreciate something, once it's widely accepted by the who's who.

So, here's an indigenous version of your very own breed of the confused millennial, spoiled for choices but doesn't know if she can choose or she is the chosen one.

~s~c~m~

~ ~ MY MERAKI NOTES ~ ~

2. Happyholic or Workoholic

Let me start by quoting something of my own, from a post I had shared on Facebook in December 2020.

The LAST Lap of 2020

The #countdownbegins. A digit will change from 0 to 1 and suddenly, we will be sprung into a whole new year. For a 4.5-billion-year-old Earth, this change is probably as small as rounding of some decimals here and there. But, for us, it's a whole new-everything.

The year 2020 shook up a lot of things for a lot of people - for good, for bad. As they say, some things need to be shaken up, some things need to be displaced, to create space for the new.

While some people lost livelihoods, some actually quit their jobs and took a leap of faith to follow their calling. People joined hands and work got divided into cooking, doing dishes, doing laundry and what not. People wore masks and gears and marched to work on duty-calls. People operated remotely and filled in for their WFH hours.

People lived without luxuries they had mistaken for needs. People realized how much we had taken life for granted.

Most of all, people realized that every time we complained for what we didn't have, somebody somewhere was praying and begging for what we have.

People started being grateful for their blessings.

I realized #alloftheabove and I am an equal representation of all of the above. I have started taking some disciplined efforts about #whatreallymatters to me. **Ask yourself this, "…if you have just #24hours to live right from this hour, what is that one thing you would want to accomplish?"**

I got my answer and that's exactly what I am doing if I have only one day to live.

I will write. That's my superpower.

We are all blessed with one. We need to seek it, tap into it and give back as we grow.

I don't know if life is fragile or not, but I do know that a flower is fragile, but as long as it lives, it does what it is meant to do – spread fragrance.

So, how differently are you going to plan the next year? How casual are you going to be?

Life will always come around with that #silverlining of all those 31st Decembers, wherein we will consider it a fresh start (but sadly only to fall back to the older patterns) but why wait till the fag end of the day, of the week, of the month, of years together to realize what truly matters.

We humans like it when things don't come easy to us, we probably like the feeling of having fought for it, that's how we probably feel it's worthy. It's like we don't value freedom until someone takes it away from us. We have history supporting this - monarchies, battles, wars.

It has always taken an external force to put away internal differences and unite people towards a common cause.

Crowned-men have always ruled fellow-men and subjected them to atrocities; only this time it was a crowned-virus that got the better of us. And I guess, it made us realize a lot of things. **For me, my most precious learning was – that the time is now or never.**

I don't know why but it felt to me like I was sitting on a throbbing volcano during the lockdown. That volcano was my own suppressed feelings, emotions, wishes, ifs and buts, what if – all the chances that I didn't take because I was busy saying Yes to other things in life, other things that were hammered into me – study, get a job, get promotions, get married, have kids etc - what if, I never get them back, what if I have lost my chance forever.

My only ask is, what have you realized in this time when you were locked-down? What have you discovered about yourself that probably scares the shit out of you?

Did you feel the pressure that time is running out,
the world might come to an end and you didn't
even try doing what you wanted to do,
you didn't even try to 'get a scratch'
of the things that are meant for you?

Right now, the vaccine we need the most is #humanvaccine – the realisation that we are so much more than the barriers we have put for ourselves and we don't need two doses – do we – 2020 was hell of a dose, already!

So, like or not, share or not, copy paste or not, if you are reading this and felt an #energyshift, you just got vaccinated with #humanvaccine and there are no phase-wise vaccination drives, because everyone is a potential-beneficiary – so just #passontheenergy in whichever way you can and let's get more and more people vaccinated with #humanvaccine.

Caution: The only side-effect (the best ever side effect) is that you will start living each day as if you only have 24 hours to live and will start doing what really matters. Spread your #uniquefragrance.

~s~c~m~

Well, you know what guys?

Honest confession: Despite me writing this piece, despite me this close to realizing a few things, it took me yet another year to finally take that plunge. It's 2022 already!

So, what's your take away from this? What is that one thing you will do (of course apart from spending time with your loved ones) if all you have is 24 hours to live, beginning right now!

The clock is ticking. Yes. You have the answer.

It's the first thing that came to your mind,
without you applying all the filters,
all the subconscious/society-fitted filters.

Just like when a car is manufactured, some features are company-fitted, most of our insecurities and inhibitions are born with us, as accumulations of the past-life-karmas and our society does a good job in nurturing that little seed into a huge tree, making you, just like them, cars manufactured in a factory.

If by chance, you are able to stand apart and realize, you want a CNG too along with the company-fitted-petrol, people will raise eyebrows. It's a different thing, they will appreciate you (probably) when you are able to save few bucks on long drives, but not without the taunts that go along while waiting inside the car in CNG queues (this was a scenario in early 2010-2015, at least where I lived, on the fringes on Mumbai, in Dombivli.

So, if I have digressed you enough, that you aren't filtering anymore, do you have the no-filter-answer? Say it, just say it aloud.

Say it aloud without being afraid, without judging yourself, without lacing it with worries of whether or not it's possible.

Say it, just say it – be honest with yourself, that's the least you can do. Don't shove that answer with logic of - *but kaise, magar kyu, kya ye possible hai.*

I understand, most of you have responsibilities and even if heart in heart you want to do what you want to do, you are making sacrifices.

So, one thing we all accept, that sacrifice is something that one has to make, growing up. Well, my suggestion is, why not make it a friend and put it to some use, ask it some favors.

I understand you probably can't pursue a career of that secret-wish/desire of yours. But, can you find time, 30 minutes a day (15 minutes in the morning, 15 minutes in the night), for yourself to spend with that secret-wish?

If you have accepted sacrificing your entire life doing a job you don't love, sacrificing 30 minutes from things like over-sleeping, procrastination, laziness, Instagram, Netflix etc. is hardly a sacrifice.

Probably, nothing will happen in terms of you making it big in that area. Probably something could. There's always a 50% chance on both sides. But, there's a 100% chance that you will find yourself a little happier - with yourself. Imagine being just 1% happier each day with 30 minutes of magic.

Imagine, this time, next year, after a year of accumulated happiness.

Can there be a bigger bliss than being satisfied with yourself? Don't you want to raise your happiness quotient? When you are happy, whether or not you want it you are going to leave a happy trail, wherever you are, with whoever you are. Initially with a consistent inside out push, this entire process will reach a flow-state wherein, not-being-happy, will be out of your control. How's that sounding!!!!

Although the majority of people will fall into this category, where they can't genuinely give up on their responsibilities and only spend 30 minutes of their time, there's a more majority of those who are trapped in their minds, more than with responsibilities.

It's not that, if they don't keep on doing the job they hate, they wouldn't get to eat, sleep, go to movies once in a while. But they are plagued with the evil called, *'what will others say'*– like I said, I am sure some of you out there have genuine responsibilities and like I also said, I am sure so many of you are into that viscous cycle because of what others might say and it's not just about what they actually will say as much as it is about you 'worrying' what they might say, think, feel, about you.

Take time out and maybe ask yourself these questions:

- What is the worst-case scenario or best-case scenario?

____

____

____

____

____

____

- What would you choose to do with your time if all your basic needs of food, clothing, shelter were taken care of?

____

____

____

____

____

____

- What would you do with your time if you never had to worry about money?

____

____

____

____

____

____

- What are those things that make you forget time, lose track of time because you are so involved doing it?

____

____

____

____

____

____

- When was the last time you lost track of time?

____

____

____

____

____

____

- What are the things or that one topic you can talk about for hours?

____

____

____

____

____

____

- What are the things or that one thing you will never be bored of doing?

____

____

____

____

____

____

- What is that one thing/s that always rejuvenates you, never exhausts you?

____

____

____

____

____

____

- What are you obsessed about in life?

____

____

____

____

____

____

- What gives you a kick in life? (expect drugs)

____

____

____

____

____

____

- What is that one thing you will ask for if God grants you a wish?

____

____

____

____

____

____

- What is that one thing you will do if you had just one day to live?

____

____

____

____

____

____

- What is that one thing you will do if you were to be immortal?

____

____

____

____

____

____

- Who would you pick to be if God grants you to live like your favorite person for a day?

____

____

____

____

____

____

~s~c~m~

Here's one incident.

I had a colleague, who loved his job, who was a workaholic. So much so, he liked working 12-15 hours a day. Of course, it's a nice thing to be passionate. Even I was impressed with his dedication. But eventually, as we spent work-time together, as I started understanding the business better, I realized it took me 7-8 hours to finish what he took 12-15 hours to complete.

No, it's not exactly about efficiency, I am talking about. Nor the quality of work or output. It's about how much you are working vs how much you are 'showing' that you are working.

It's about productivity and time-management. It not about how much you can accomplish in one hour vs how better you can do if you have two hours for the same task. It's about how much time you need to spend on that one task in a day given that there are fifty more tasks that need your time. It's always about plotting and planning.

- Most important
- Most urgent
- Important but not urgent
- Urgent but not important for that day

I am surely in for spending 10 hours a day even 15 hours a day when needed; some days are such when you have to stretch. But on most days, you can wind up work, quality work with 7-8 hours a day. I loved my job too but people always assumed because he punched in more hours, he had more work to do; whereas we both almost always had the same amount of work.

Just that, I also had a life outside of my job – I loved to spend time reading, writing, traveling and being with my family too – doesn't mean I loved my job any lesser; it only meant I knew how to plot the 'important-urgent' quadrant.

We humans love it when things don't come easy; we feel that only when we stretch, do we deserve success. And I am all game for stretching, but I am in for the kind of stretching that builds me up, not breaks me down.

Builds me up in all walks of life that matter. What usually happens is, stretching for long hours at work means no time for workout or meditation or pursuing hobbies; which means inviting health problems for the future, falling into the work-imbalance trap.

So, circling back to that office colleague, this is what happened, one day -

Since we were on good talking terms, I asked him because I had started feeling bad about how he had let his mind trap him. I was even willing to give him the benefit of doubt that he didn't know what he was doing to himself.

I ask him, trying to mince my words as much as I could, not trying to be mean or rude or judgemental or preachy (only out of concern) - "What do you do on weekends or rather what were your hobbies before you started working?"

He begins saying that, for starters, most of his weekends are also occupied with work but then he gives me a laundry list of things he used to love doing back in school/college. And his eyes beam with the memory of it.

I couldn't help myself ask him, "Wow, you looked so happy just talking about it. You must be pursuing few of these even today."

And he says the three golden words, *"Time kaha hai!"* It's never about *time kaha hai* (for most of us), it's always about *'how important it really is'*– if it's important you will make time, isn't it?

I mean I tried to tell him about my 30 minutes per day formula but he always had something or the other as a come-back – boss, meeting, presentations – so on and so forth. All I could do was smile, after a certain point. I had to stop myself from convincing him. Because you can't force it on anyone. If I could convince him, about just one thing, I would like to tell him and many more like him;

"Kitna kuch try karte hai hum life hai,
yeh bhi try kar lo! It might just work!"

What's the harm in trying out that 30 minutes formula? Max to max, it won't work, but then at least you tried. But what if it starts working? What is you start feeling more fulfilled and happy?

I know this from experience, this is some deep-rooted shit, I have been through it too. Sometimes when things actually fall in place, we suddenly seem to not-know what do to, how to receive it! Because, all our lives we are so used to chasing, getting used to something actually happening can take a while.

I also know one more thing - only when you are ready, when it's time, only when you are truly seeking, will change happen.

Me trying to convince him after a point, was me losing out on my energy. Trust me, such things can't be forced unless one has the inclination on his own.

You will meet the kind of people who will act as catalysts, you will have instances in your life filled with opportunities, you will automatically choose what is right for you; you will get every possible sign from the Universe, only when you are truly ready – to fly.

I have met people who have acted as catalysts, and I felt it was my responsibility to try to be one for someone else, share what I received when I needed it. That got me thinking and it's one of the reasons that motivated me to take this up :)

~s~c~m~

Here's one more story, a video I saw on YouTube.

One day, in a class of 30 odd kids of grade 5 or 6, a teacher decides to play some interactive games. The kids enjoy the session very much.

At the end of the session, the class teacher distributes a plain paper and a color pen to every student. She then turns to the blackboard and writes this Q there – *'What do you want to be when you grow up?'*

She asks the students to write the answer to this Q and display the paper over their heads for her to see.

Some of them have traditional answers like Doctor, Engineer, Lawyer etc; some of them are unconventional answers like YouTuber, Gamer, Actor, Writer etc. But there's one answer that leaves the teacher confused.

She applauds everyone's answer and dismisses the class. However, she asks that one student to wait behind.

She goes up to the student and asks him with concern as to why did he write what he wrote. Did he not understand the meaning of the question on the blackboard? She tries to explain to him the kind of answers that were expected by giving examples of other students and their answers.

The student looks at the teacher with innocent questioning eyes and replies, "Teacher, my mother is a doctor, my father is a lawyer, my elder brother is studying engineering and everyday at the dinner table they all crib and complain about how their lives are. So many times, we don't even have dinner together. Makes me wonder if they are all sad. Are you also sad, teacher? All I want to do when I grow up is be happy, with whatever I do."

He continues earnestly, "I don't quite know what I will be growing up. One day I want to be a doctor but the very next day I feel like becoming a dancer. It's very confusing to me. But the common quotient in both scenarios is I see myself smiling – be it as a doctor or a dancer. So, that means, I can be whatever makes me happy, can't I?"

"Of course, you can be whatever you want to be and be happy with whatever you become!" is all the teacher could say. She is utterly spell bound with the reply. She now understands why he wrote HAPPY on the plain paper when others wrote different things.

Sadhguru often says that, formal education can do more harm than help and ain't this a perfect example! If you happen to have kids around you, try to learn how they see life, try to do that before formal education corrupts them! There's learning everywhere if the learner wants to learn.

Our conditioning is such that we only feel these labels, tags etc. will make us happy. Ask yourself, who you are without your name, tag, designation?

I have asked this question a lot when I used to conduct workshops. And it used to always lead to a riot - confusions, discussions but always ended up being the most self-revealing question.

So, what are you waiting for? Go find some self-revelation, find your happiness quotient. Share with me if you are a workaholic or happyholic. You may reach out to me on my Instagram Handle @themerakiwoman. Hoping to get a lot of DMs there!

~s~c~m~

~ ~ MY MERAKI NOTES ~ ~

3. Get Fascinated with Yourself.

I have spent lot of summer holidays at my maternal uncle's place.

Like every other Indian family, all of us cousins, little 5- or 6-year-olds would be asked to 'showcase' our talent. All the uncles and aunts, *didis* and *bhaiyas* would circle around us post lunchtime and make us dance to Bollywood numbers.

I remember, all of them would laugh their guts out because we all were such wonderful performers. We too, loved doing that because what followed this were rounds of *ice-golas*, kulfis, colas and every other thing that was banned to us kids, during the non-summer-holidays.

I was the chubbiest kid in the house, needless to say I was super-cute and my chubbiness and cuteness not only landed me with lots of kisses and cheek-pulls but also extra helpings of everything – mangoes, jamuns, kulfis, *golas, imlis, bor,* etc.

Today when we all recall those days, while making the next set of little 5- or 6-year-olds undergo the same drill, we too have a good laugh because, we realize the whole objective of making them dance, is to see their innocent, funny, (in my case) chubby moves.

Back then it used to fascinate me, how I would unknowingly make everyone laugh. It was always the motivation behind me being dance-ready – making people laugh! But today if someone asks me to do that I will be extremely awkward, my dancing skills are not only minus, but my hand-leg coordination is like spiders crawling - it's everywhere.

Back then also, my dance was always spidery, just that, there was no worry about 'what people would say' and even if they said something, it was more about 'having fun yourself'. Back then, didn't we all want to grow up fast, be like that one *didi* or *bhaiya* everyone adored? Well, who knew that what they wanted was to become one of us again! Care-free and happy!

The very thing that motivated me to dance back then, haunts me today – people would laugh! There's so much less baggage when we are kids, it's easy to be fascinated about everything - new experiences, new people, new places, new clothes, new books, new toys, new everything - small joys.

Why do we leave behind those things, growing up? Rather, why do we leave behind the good things? What changes? And why?

~s~c~m~

Getting fascinated with yourself?

What exactly does this mean?
Let me rather ask, are you fascinated with yourself?

Well, this is a tricky ask; especially because I know so many people who are so fascinated with themselves but are a bunch of assholes, absolute hypocrites. At the same time, there's a whole bunch out there who in reality are kick-ass people, but will probably always undermine their self-worth and be fascinated with the first half of people, instead of being fascinated about who they are.

We as a society have always glamorized one subset of qualities, natures, traits, behaviors over other. For example, the outgoing ones are considered more fun, more approachable, more friendly while conveniently labeling the non-outgoing ones as shy, boring, reserved or even rude!

The summer days as kids were fun, because the fact that people were laughing didn't matter. I was always the shy and introverted kind but I still was curious about life, fascinated with things, observant about how people behaved, why they behaved so etc. I was open to possibilities; I was quite full of life and innocence.

As I grew up, the shyness and introverted-ness remained but the fascination was replaced by fear - fear of being judged, fear of not fitting in, fear of being laughed at. Subconsciously we are learning so much that we start telling ourselves, it's best not to fall, so people won't laugh, it's best not to fail so people won't judge, it's best not to try anything new, anything out of the box so that there's no question of falling or failing, thus no question of people laughing or judging.

I mean, we become the victims of this 'fitting-in monster' so much that we choose to fail doing 'what is accepted' over failing by 'trying something new.' Cliched example, but only to make the point clearer; we prefer to choose at failing trying to become a doctor, lawyer, engineer, corporate dummies (because it's a profession that is more accepted) than choosing to fail in the area that excites us like maybe becoming a singer, dancer, painter, writer, an RJ or maybe a tattoo artist, plethora of off-beat options here (sadly the non-so-commonly accepted ones.)

We choose to stay mediocre doing the things we don't like to do than choosing to learn with failures in the things we want to do and eventually master it. See, this might seem repetitive but like we discussed some time back, we got to choose our pain, our struggle, our failures. What I mean by this is – let's say I decide to become a tattoo artist, I will still have to put in painful hours of practise, I will still have to go through the struggle of finding the right guidance or mentors and I will still fail many times before becoming a fine tattoo artist – but all this will be worth it because at end of the day, I know that, every single day makes me happy, makes me full, makes me whole.

Most of the successful people out there, what do you think really keeps them going?

Money? Power? Fame?

All these are by-products of what really
keeps them going and
what really keeps them going is,
they do what fuels the fire within their souls.

I love to quote SRK on this, that, the way he wants to leave this world someday (God bless him with a long, healthy, happy life) will be on stage, doing a part, performing a role. **'This' - if you find 'this' for yourself, you are sorted.**

Now the question arises, as to how does one 'narrow down' on 'this.' I will probably not be the best person for this because it took me a decade of finally narrowing down to 'this.' And in the same decade I also spent months and years staying mad at myself because I wasn't able to narrow it down earlier, because after doing a job or learning something for some time – I would kind of get bored, I would want to try something else.

Trust me I can write an entire chapter on the list of things, I tried and eliminated. But see, that's the thing. There are all kinds of people in the world – some know it like the back of their hand, what they want to dedicate their life to, while for some it's the back of the back! Hope you got the pun! Sorry, bad one :D

And for me, I did a lot of 'beating myself up' for being so non-constant, for being such a variable because I ALWAYS had one person as my frame of comparison.

That person being my partner – my first ever friend, my first ever boyfriend and now my husband. He is way too sorted, way to perfect and when I 'accuse' him of being so, he has this answer ready – *I am not perfect, I too have imperfections, I just work on it every day* – and this is exactly the kind of thing a perfect, sorted person will say (I miss the rolling eyes emoji so much, right now!)

Just because he took to numbers and everything related to numbers, like a fish takes to water doesn't mean everyone arrives at their calling in the first go. Maybe I always wanted to write. Maybe I took my first step towards it when I published my first book in 2014 titled Romantic Resonance by Leadstart; that too after taking a sabbatical from work for almost a year. Maybe I did show some balls, to pursue what I felt was right for me rather than logic ruling out the magic of how it wasn't going to be a right monetary-decision.

And logic won. A year of no income, sufficiently good response for the book – a Radio Mirchi 98.3 interview by none other than 'the' Jeeturaj, handwritten review by Agneepath director, Karan Malhotra and genuine positive feedback by readers.

But yet, instead of pursuing it further with belief in my writing, I made myself believe that I was an average writer if I wasn't earning – and I decided to go back to 9 to 5!

And maybe I was an average writer
and maybe I wasn't
– who knew – I never gave myself that
second chance –
neither with persistence on the marketing
effort on the first book
nor trying to write the next book.

Like I said, I have a laundry list of things I did juggling the 9 to 5 (and we all know, it's never a 9 to 5 - it's always a 9 to 9 thingy) but always slept with a certain helplessness, restlessness. Until 2020 happened, until I started penning down this.

So, about 'narrowing' down – there's only one way to find out – try out things, it's okay to do that – but don't be mad at yourself while you are doing that, don't keep comparing yourself with your peers, siblings etc. – be your own force, your own critic, your own support – and remember that elimination is a sure shot way towards decluttering – towards understanding what to say No to – so as to make space and say Yes for what matters – what is meant to happen to you. **You will grow in your career only if you grow as an individual.**

Also, a small hack is that, most of the time, your real calling will circle around what made you happy as a child.

Just to conclude on this – most of the times the worst part is we go so far ahead in this journey of doing safe-things, being just-another person, we realize not until it's too late that, that, maybe we never even gave ourself the time, the chance to find out what is that thing we really like to do more than anything else.

Take a few minutes pause here, internalize if this has happened with you.

~s~c~m~

Maybe this book is not for you, if you don't relate to what I am saying, it's for someone like me, for my own younger self back then. Maybe I speak for myself; but I so wish I had this book, this self-awareness growing up. So that I would have been less hard on myself, less critical about my inherent nature; so that I would have invested my energy in grooming my authentic nature than diverting it to becoming someone else just because it was commonly accepted.

But, let me tell you something, something, that is the current scenario.

These days, I am very much fascinated with myself, and I have come a long way from one side of the pendulum to the other, from one belief-system to the other.

I love what I am becoming because I have lost too much not valuing myself sooner.

Remember that scene from the Bollywood movie, 3 idiots, where, in the interview round Sharma Joshi tells the panel of interviewers, "*dono tange tudwa ke apne pairon ke khada rehna sikha hai, sir, badi mushkil se aya hai yeh attitude….*"

Something like that is my story too, haven't literally ended up breaking my legs, but have lost a lot before gaining this mindset (and yes, I did end up having a hairline leg fracture). I have hated myself a lot, circled a lot on that vicious circle of self-loathing, self-doubt, self-blame, self-criticism before arriving at a place where all I have for myself is 'self-love.'

Self-love doesn't mean, you don't make mistakes or everything just becomes perfectly flawless,
it just means that you take effort in the direction of becoming a better version of yourself.

You see the flaws, you accept the flaws, you take steps towards bettering some, towards living with some because they aren't really flaws, they are just like lazy-muscles on a cheek that could be a potential dimple.

Self-hate meant you hated yourself when you made a mistake and instead of taking effort to learn from it, it always ended up in a demotivating self-dialogue – things like 'I am not good enough', 'I am such an idiot', 'I screw up every time', 'I don't deserve anything good', 'I am a failure', 'I am letting everyone down', 'I will never be successful', 'I will always be a disappointment', 'I don't trust myself anymore', 'I am sure I will screw up the next time also', 'Why don't I ever learn' etc. etc.

I always had this mixed inferiority-superiority complex. And it's not easy to admit what I am going to in the next few paras. But, I will because that is what inner-work is, that is what self-discovery looks like. And I had mentioned sometime back that sometimes self-discovery sucks, but, in the right stride, it is a step closer to self-awareness and thus self-improvement.

To be fascinated with yourself in the most authentic way is to first see the mirror - admit, acknowledge the flaws – flaws in thoughts, flaws in approach, attitude - to give away that what is not you and make space for the real you.

Okay so, here goes.

I grew up in an extremely loved and protected environment. Being the only child, I was always the center of attention. No, I was never a fussy kid who demanded attention (if that's what you are thinking) but I almost always got it nevertheless.

Just that, I grew up believing that everywhere I go, I will always be cared for as much, given the first preference and what not. So somehow, I grew up with very poor social skills because, for everything I needed, my parents were my go-to-people. I barely had 2 friends that too, because they all lived in my building, we went to the same school, studied in the same class.

I was basically caught up in a small pool with only two people being my frame of reference for everything – which translates to less exposure to people of my age, people of other varied age groups. One of my biggest shortcomings from this not-at-all-intentionally done upbringing-mistake is – having a myopic perspective on most things – in the most formative stages of behavior and personality.

When I stepped out of my protected cocoon and went to college, I was in for a huge slap, there were dozens of things people my age were doing or had already done which I was being told that, *'these are the things grown-ups do'*.

As my people-exposure increased, I was in a shock as to how different the world can be in comparison to my earlier close-knit world. Everything suddenly multiplied – the struggle to fit it, the desperation to change to a more like-able version. I had not even formed a personality to be able to understand if I wanted to change it or not and even if it had to change, to what it should change.

We often hear people say this, *'be yourself, be comfortable in your skin.'*

But for me, suddenly, it was '*Who am I' exactly? Am I what I was told I was for over 2 decades of my life or was I someone who was liking the possibilities of what I could be as I started meeting new people?'*

One realization that has dawned upon me today is that – maybe people in their twenties should stay outside of the comfort of their homes for some years, maybe for studies or maybe for a job; at least for a year or two. You are suddenly outside of the influence of your folks, your relatives – a new place, new people, new experiences – it does loads in helping you discover yourself.

So, circling back to 'be yourself, be comfortable in your skin' – for a long time and by long, I mean till almost three decades of my life, I didn't know who I was as an individual, I didn't know who I was outside the comfort of my people, my parents, my partner. Because as soon as I started college, I found someone, we started dating and since then, my world has always been my parents and my partner.

And hence, I had a hard time, feeling fascinated about myself, because I was constantly pendulating between what I was told I was and what I had started to realize about who I was.

Trust me, no one actively coerced me as don't do this, don't do that; just that I had seen and passively absorbed that to be decently happy in life, one must make safe choices. And that I guess has been an upbringing ritual ingrained in every middle-class family – be scared – be scared to be happy, be scared to live fully, be scared of being rich, be scared of doing anything unconventional – and I don't mean that it's what they are doing on purpose – it's so ingrained that they don't even know they are doing it – it's a part of their subconscious system as well – driving them to do it like habits.

There's a saying in Marathi, *'Shivaji janmala yava tar shejarcha gharat.'* It means that, our folks keep giving us examples of great mean, the likes of Chhatrapati Shivaji Maharaj and/or let's say late Kalpana Chawla or even Master Blaster Sachin Tendulkar – but tomorrow if you and I were to fail standard 10th like Sachin did – do you think our parents will allow us to pursue Cricket!

You get the drift, right? So, our folks will want Einsteins being made out of us, as long as we get a fixed salary every month, come back home on time, marry on time, reproduce on time, be in the safe zone and get wow-things done!

I have a friend who wanted to pursue acting and he was allowed to do that only after he finished his engineering. He told me that, his parents felt, by the time he completed engineering, *uska acting-bhoot utar jaega!* But that didn't happen and it makes me proud of his determination that he made it in quite a few Marathi films and serials.

This sort of happened to me also. My entire family (my parents, my then boyfriend, his parents) had gone to watch this Marathi Film – *Harishchandra chi Factory*. It is a biographical film based on the life of Dadasaheb Phalke who is the Father of Indian Cinema. All of us loved the movie and spoke at length about how one needs madness to achieve something as exceptional as this and how we are all always aiming for something small, instead of giving it all and aiming for the stars.

I was glued to every scene; every dialogue and that film will always stay with me because it made me realize something – something like a Eureka moment. It made me realize my crazy love for stories – in the form of movies. I have always loved stories in the form of novels and this movie-thing was a discovery.

Breaks my heart to mention this, but some days after the movie, while I was in my first job, I announced to my family, out of nowhere over lunch that – I wanted to pursue writing full time. My parents, who are usually supportive about things, looked at me and then looked at my (future) in-laws who were sitting across the table with questions in their eyes. It was a time, when my partner and I had finished our studies, had started earning and had decided to make our relation official to our respective parents.

No one said anything directly but their silence said a lot of things and without getting into details of what was being told to me and by whom, they convinced me it was a foolish idea that won't pay me a dime, it was way too risky to leave such a good paying job, it would look erratic on my resume if I quit my first job to pursue something as uncertain as writing!

These were the same people who had unanimously agreed to having a certain amount of madness to be able to achieve something out of the world!

'Shivaji Theory' hence proved.

I wanted to respond and defend but I didn't, I couldn't. However, the urge to write a novel was so strong that, a couple years later I did quit my job and wrote my first book – Romantic Resonance. I did take that first step but did not take the next step after the first step.

After a few months of getting the book published, I sort of gave up on it because I was increasingly being told things like, 'look at your peers, they are earning and getting promoted', 'don't you have any financial responsibility' etc. etc.

I could have pursued, used my marketing degree to market my book (one of the publishing mistakes I did, which today I count as a 'missed learning opportunity' and not a mistake). To cut the long story short, I went back to a 9 to 5 even more scared than before to take another leap of faith.

Scared because, I did something half-way but concluded that I was a failure.
Scared because, I gave a chance to others to keep taunting me with 'I had told you so, don't quit the job, all these dreams are not for us.'
Scared because, I went deeper into the dirt of self-doubt, loss of confidence.
Scared because, it led me to believe that life is a calculation of 2 plus 2 is a 4 and it can never be magical with 2 plus 2 being 22.
Scared because, I felt, I failed myself, I didn't try enough, not only did I not try enough, I didn't have it at all – I was less than ordinary.
Scared because, I started believing that all this writing, novels, movies is for an elite class, not for me.

~s~c~m~

I went back to my job, tried to be good at it. I was fortunate to meet some good people and work at some good places, but a part of me was always missing, always lost, always seeking, always searching for myself in those words, in those pages, in every book I read, I every movie I saw.

Lockdown was a revelation, it just gave me a push, a free-fall and made me realize half of the things we think we want we don't need them – so many material things we want to accumulate we can actually live without it, that too happily.

I am not saying in any way that one should not earn and make money, what I mean is, there is a way to do that, by doing the things you love, by investing time in the things that make you glow different.

With time on hand to think, rather to not-think,
with time on hand to introspect,
an alarm set off inside me – like a time bomb,
tick tick tick!

What if I don't ever get another chance?
What if something happens to me?
When will I really live my dream life, in reality, not just in my dreams?

What will be the worst case scenario – I might fail again, but this time I will use it as a learning!

What could be the best-case scenario – I can write another book/books/screenplay/screenplays/song/songs – what not!
How will I know, if I don't invest time on writing?

I can reach out to people with the stories, with the message and in some way make a difference, make an impact.

What for was I postponing living my life –
the way that makes my heart sing,
the way that makes my mind perform a cartwheel,
free, happy, unobstructed with my own limiting
thoughts, with eyes only on possibilities,
on what can go right for me, instead
of worrying about what could go wrong.

Like we discussed, it wasn't going to be easy, but I was willing to choose the area of struggle and make it worthy!
And it's been almost a decade since that day, when I wrote my first book, I have taken yet another plunge, yet another leap of faith!

I do have a list of writing projects I am currently working on, but I have started off with this because I don't want yet another Ketaki/Ketan to take yet another decade to arrive at this decision. You know what I mean!

To be good at anything, the most important thing that you need is to give it the time it needs to nurture itself, the sooner the better.

I won't push you saying Start TODAY, but I will insist, Start SOONER.

Take your time to arrive at this decision, be in a flow state when you make that decision.

Arrive at by yourself not because I am saying Yes or someone else is saying No.

Make that decision from a place of self-awareness and not desperation or agitation or rebellion. It's easier said than done. I know. So, as of now on an immediate basis, do nothing, just breathe in and breathe out and tell yourself this –

I am one step closer to making the right decision for myself.
I am exactly where I need to be.
I am on the path that I am supposed to be, meant to be
The forces are with me.

Just remember to tell yourself this, every single day - I am fascinated with myself with the efforts I am taking on myself and this time next year I will be a lot closer to the person I have always wanted to be.

Before you proceed to the next chapter, make yourself a promise, with today's date and a date this time, next year.

Today's Date: ____________________
This Time Next Year: _____________________

My Promise to Myself:

____

____

____

~s~c~m~

~ ~ MY MERAKI NOTES ~ ~

4. Balance the Effort with Surrender...

There's always an eerie feeling associated with superheroes and superpowers, isn't it? Why this fascination for something fictional?

Or is it that 'fiction' is something real but unrealized that takes it to a completely different pedestal?

Carl Jung talks about something called 'collective unconscious'. That fascination and mad belief in the existence of a superhero often stems from one's collective unconscious – which is a home to layers of suppressed feelings, hidden emotions, unaddressed fears – everything nameless, shapeless, logicless – to the rational mind.

All of this eventually finds expression in some or the other form evolving from signs, symbols and scriptures to capes, spiderwebs and racer cars. Today that super power has yet another name that is, digitalization.

After decoding the psychological aspect of 'origin of a superhero', I have understood that a superhero is in fact the most ordinary girl/guy who – realizes his power and chooses to use it responsibly, thus making him 'super.'

You don't have to necessarily wear a cape or spew out a spiderweb to be a superhero. Because the cape and spiderweb is symbolic of their power. What is symbolic of your power can be anything and everything - a painting, a dance performance, a java script, a html coding, an essay, a speech, a sales target, a spacecraft, teaching, stand-up comedy, digital marketing - you name it and you can be it.

A superhero is every person who can make a difference in this world with the superpower they have.

All you got to do is find your unique power and make it your superpower.

A superhero is not someone out there who will come to your rescue.

A superhero is the person who is reading this right now and getting ready to rescue others, by wearing his symbolic cape, his superpower – because he/she has rescued himself/herself in the first place by finding out about their own superpower.

Took me a while to arrive, fully embrace and surrender to my superpower. Needless to call it aloud, but nevertheless I still will because, it is what makes me me, what sort of completes me – it is this power of writing – which for the longest time, I never acknowledged as my gift.

When I say, writing is my superpower, it's more than just being fascinated by it, it's almost like my need – just like it is to eat, sleep, breathe. And we all are blessed with one such super power, it's just that it's either dormant or it's just lost below the clutter of hundreds of things we do every day.

And yes, yet another very important reason as to why writing is my superpower, is that, I grew up on words of lot of writers and they kept me going, they almost always answered the questions I couldn't even frame properly as a question – and if that is the power of words – I want to do my bit and maybe give back in my way, with the gift of writing – **I am sure one word at a time, one person at a time, this world can be a better place.**

~s~c~m~

As a writer, as I dedicate time to write this, glue this together, I have quit my full-time job and I really don't know what and where I will be a year from now (it's March 2022 right now)

All I know is I have some savings that will help me survive for a while.
All I know is I need to write this book because it's been giving me sleepless nights.
All I know is I need to give it the time it needs to take it to completion.
All I know right now is that this is the immediate next step.

And yes, I am blessed that my family supports me in this journey financially, to some extent emotionally – I say 'to some extent' because they will give me all the support they can, **but let's face it, no one can really push it for you, no one can do what you must do on your own.**

As mentioned in our previous conversations, I believe that, for now, all I have to do is trust what I know *in-the-moment*, put in genuine effort and allow the Forces to guide me. One needs to balance the effort with absolute faith in surrender.

Let me share something.
I had a friend, who was far more talented, far more hard working, far more disciplined, far more kind than most others in the peer group. And most of the time, he got what he wanted, what he planned on getting.

However, in comparison to another friend who was talented, who worked hard, who was also jolly and easy going, who practiced gratitude, who found time to pursue his passion apart from work, the former friend always seemed to get less than he deserved.

Well, this has been my observation not just for them, but when I reflected, I realized I was also behaving like the former friend.

Sometimes, we take life way too seriously, we plan too much, we miss that we also need to go easy, try not to control too much, so much that it suffocates. More than anything, we miss the chance to let life guide us towards things that we haven't possibly dreamt of because LIFE has such a bigger understanding than us!

I had seen a reel wherein a very popular influencer by the name *mostlysane* was narrating a conversation she had with my favorite person on Earth, i.e, Sadhguru. I am sure, Sadhguru, needs no introduction.

A shocked Prajakta Kohli (mostlysane) reacts to Sadhguru telling her, "May you never get what you dream to be."

"Why would someone ever say that!" she exclaims.

Sadhguru laughs his signature childlike-life-reverberating-laugh and responds, "May you be so much more than you can ever dream to be."

See, that's the power of surrender.

But, again, it is very easy to fall into the trap of 'how much should the effort be' before surrendering? It is very easy to get wronged and maybe 'work too less or too hard and not take the right amount of effort' before finding the sweet spot between Effort and Surrender.

And for this, there's one pro-tip that can get you started with.

This comes from one of Ankur Warikoo's reels (my second most favorite person - again, the man needs no introduction) and he has also mentioned about this in his book 'Do Epic Shit.'

One of the things I write in my goal book is 'I want to be like him when I hit 40.'

Well, he says (and I am using my own interpretation here) – **one should focus on building habits rather than fixating on goals**.

In the path of reaching a goal, there are external and internal factors both. External being obviously circumstances beyond your control – covid 19 for example. Internal being obviously how you handle the external situations, how you push yourself, pep yourself etc.

So, basically a goal is subject to certain amount of variability plus the added amount of stress! But habit is a constant-something you do every day, with discipline, with an aim towards reaching that goal and after an X amount of time of **'being in a certain habit'** you are bound to reach from point A to point B. This point B can be somewhat closer to your goal or it could be the exact goal or if you are extra lucky, even beyond your goal. But you are bound to move in the forward direction.

The point being, a good habit will surely take you where you want to be, it's only a matter of time – and the best part is you get to enjoy the process while keeping an eye on the goal, instead of negatively stressing yourself out by being fixated on the goal.

I believe some of you are also fixated on the luck factor that I have just mentioned. Most successful people often talk about 'creating your own luck' and while it's a fact that 'the more you work, the luckier you get'; I also believe in some amount of divine intervention – commonly called 'luck factor.' And this comes from all your previous births' accumulated karmas.

Your previous lives-karmas decide to whom you are born to, your parents, your culture, your nationality, your inclination to certain things more than certain other things, your genetic predisposition – the list can go on.

Many people reading this may or may not agree to this or our human intellect/ego may not want to acknowledge the presence of the divine and I leave it up to them to agree or disagree.

In my opinion, most people either fall prey to too much 'dependence' on the divine or are too arrogant to acknowledge the divine. Believe me when I say this because I have seen both of these extremes in my family!

There's one more person I would like to mention who strengthened my existing belief in divine intervention and that's Ranveer Allahbadia (he also holds the 'second-favorite-person' position), the face behind BeerBiceps. Umm, in my opinion or let's say exposure, I had always heard about this sort of divine intervention being spoken so openly from Western Philosophies as Law of Attraction and the likes of it.

And I am pretty sure, we have the roots to these philosophies in our culture ; but our problem is that we don't accept something unless it's Westernized; Yoga would be one more classic case. And thanks to Ranveer, he is Indian-izing it.

So going back to habit-forming, incorporating certain good practises like – meditation, exercise, eating healthy, sleeping on time, having morning rituals, restricting whiling away time by scanning the phone for no real reason, journaling, affirmation, power-tapping, ho'oponopono technique, reading self-help books like these, listening to motivating podcasts, etc. etc. will certainly help.

See, it all depends on you, how soon you find this balance – you may find none of these techniques work for you or maybe a combination work or you may invent something of your own. In addition to all this, read this amazing book called The Big Magic by Elizabeth Gilbert, if you get a chance. She has very beautifully conveyed how 'energy' chooses to have conversations with you, how you can identify the universal signs etc.

~s~c~m~

Meraki is what happens to you, when you leave a piece of your soul in anything and everything that you love to do.
And, that is precisely what makes it Unique. That makes Every person, Unique, in some way or the other. And, Humble at the same time, because nothing really is unique,

everything is Inspired from Nature and Universe.

When you surrender with *Shraddha* and *Saburi* (Faith and Patience), you are actually rising to another dimension of life.

My most valuable life lesson; everyone and everything has a place in the scheme of things. I can vouch you won't believe what I am about to say. And, I would have done the same thing had someone told me this out of thin air. Just read with an open mind, absorb like a sponge, for the time being.

What you want, in the moment, may not always be what you need in the real long run of life.

We often don't realize that we are in fact being protected when something doesn't happen the way we want it to.

I have had my fair share of fighting, arguing with myself, with my loved ones and with the Force I believe in, because certain things didn't happen the way I wanted. Trust me, today, when I look back, I realize it was for my own good. Today, when I look back and imagine, 'had that thing happened' life would have been a disaster.

I know, you are all trying to negate what I am saying. I won't be forcing you to 'understand' this, because you won't unless it's time for you too. I have been in the same place not once, but many times.

Some things are best learnt from one's experience; only then the learning will be solid.

Just keep this somewhere at the back of your mind. Keep reflecting on this whenever you are spending some 'me time' or whenever your mind just takes off as a free-soul. (It could be as routine as when you are pooping or taking a bath or it could be done more consciously, like a few minutes before you go to sleep.)

All you have to do is, initiate a self-dialogue with the 'conscious' you and slowly allow it seep into the subconscious. Your self-dialogue/prayer goes as below.

"I wish for so and so to happen, but I have complete faith in YOU (the Universe) that I will be guided and whatever happens, will be for my good."

~s~c~m~

As far as my conscious memory goes (age 8 or so) I knew this one thing, I have no idea from where I had this seeking, and for some reason I had the this right inside me ever since I was born – I knew this one thing, like the back of my hand, that –

I don't want another birth as a human or any other form. I want to pay my karmic debts in this birth only. And, while

I do that, only I will suffer for it, none of my loved ones will have to bear the brunt of it.

I am super calm and composed as I state this, but it wasn't a well-constructed thought at that age. It was something that I couldn't really address as an eight-year-old and this was one of the reasons I was also seeking belongingness from someone I could relate to.

I wasn't even aware that eight-year-olds aren't supposed to have such thoughts - imagine my plight - trying to share something like this with a fellow eight-year-old - and his/her plight, having to listen to something so deep and so complex.

Eventually, what started happening was, in my urge to be a part of the group that inner voice started getting subdued. 'Fear of being a misfit' - is a name we know now. Back then, all that mattered was playing luka-chuppi with those bunch of friends, getting invited to their birthday parties or trying to have conversations with them around which clips/hair band went well with which Barbie-outfit; when all I wanted to ask them was 'do you feel a restless energy nagging at your soul all the time.'

Let's now say that, most of the actions as an adult were a consequence of me 'running away from that restless energy' or 'trying to find someone who shared that goddamn feeling with me, only so that I tell myself, I wasn't insane or hallucinating and there was some soul who backs it up'.

This constant 'fleeting from self' led me to having a lot of 'self-acceptance' issues which eventually also led to a lot of 'self-respect' related issues and people taking me for a ride; because I felt like a misfit, I sought belongingness. I was in a self-loathing zone, not even aware that I was self-loathing.

You get where I am coming from? Self-loathing because I wasn't taking a stand for myself, for something that I had felt so strongly, so deeply, since so long! I was at a phase where punishing myself gave me some kind of peace as if I was compensating for certain things.

Maybe, had I allowed my inner voice to guide me, instead of letting the noise take over, I would have saved myself some years and taken on this journey of writing or sharing these lessons, a little earlier.

But, as I also shared what my current self-dialogue is, "I have complete faith in the Force I believe that I will be guided and whatever happens, will be for my good." So maybe, me not realizing all of that sooner, was for a reason. Maybe, this is the right time for me to realize it.

The only reason I opened up a major hidden part of my personality is not to play any victim-card because I take full responsibility for how I have turned out. I am sharing because, I want you to know – you are not alone (like I kept feeling for all these years) and you are not crazy (like I kept blaming myself to be); just that you are different and believe me, there are a lot of people like you, like me, like us.

May this 'this' was my different, my weird; yours could be something else and it's fine - so don't be hard on yourself - **accept yourself, have faith that - it is this different and this weird - that can be the ink to your pen, the color to your painting, the lyrics to your song, the rhythm to your dance.**

Believe that if you are 'different' - it's for a reason.

I am reminded of Steve Job's commencement speech at Stanford; he had said, "…you can't connect the dots going forward, you can only connect it going backward." Check out the full speech on YouTube.

~ s ~ c ~ m ~

I want to share something – a sneak peek into my next book – just to illustrate what happens when you surrender, when you become a vessel, a medium to allow the Forces to act through you. Here goes...

"Dhruv...you, we are moving too fast, I hardly know you, you barely know me, you didn't even know I am a vegetarian until few minutes back; what we only know is we like to spend time together."

"That's what marriage, right - liking to spend time together for the rest of your life." He had answers for everything. "Relax, I am not asking you to do that right away; I only wanted you to know and my parents to know, I am ready, whenever you are!"

For a moment, the way he held me with his glance, transcended me back to *him* and that scared me more because *he* had left, just like that, without even saying a bye, after having shared a nameless deep connection. I don't know what hurt me the most - his going away or his going away without me having a chance to tell him how important he had started becoming.

I don't know what seemed a bigger sacrifice - letting him go from my life and never knowing when I will see him again or seeing him slip away from me fully knowing what he meant to me, slipping away to one-night stands and bad relationships with other girl in college. I really don't know what ached more - the fact that I could sense he was doing this on purpose despite knowing the depth of our connection or the fact that he was doing this exactly because he too, was completely aware of the depth of our connection.

When Dhruv said, you are the one I want to marry - it bought back flashes of memory, where I had imagined him saying this to me, it was a memory I had buried away and although that memory was not even a memory, it was the memory of my imagination - it had felt real and surreal - and I recollect, waking up one night, all sweaty with cold feet - as if he too shared this imagination, as if he too knew this might happen someday and that's why he left - because, it was too soon for him to be with the one, because he wanted to explore himself, see the world. It suddenly occurred to me what he meant with his ritual of calling out my name and saying, 'nothing' when I asked 'what' - he actually meant, 'everything.'

I thought all of this in a fraction of a mini-second and I could measure the time because Dhruv had just made that 'cluck' sound as he socketed the seat belt and was starting to lean back. I wanted to tell Dhruv about him, but what was I supposed to tell - that I lost a friend to unprocessed feelings? Or that I thought I shared a bond with someone who I thought felt the same about me and then he went on to live his life. I brought my fingers to my temple massaging my forehead, I was starting to get that familiar feeling of wanting to block away all the light that ever was, retreat from being *the version* I had trained myself to be, to being *me*, the broken me.

My version felt empty to me and I preferred broken to empty, I preferred hurt to being trained-to-mask emotions. I wanted to be broken again, that way I at least got to be honest with myself, but here I was being dishonest to everyone else, waning every day, waiting to be full. With *him*. With him, who was nowhere to be found. I wanted to hug the Moon, ask him to take me to him, forever.

~s~c~m~

That's about it, for now. Well, I don't know if you liked it or maybe without context it's difficult to say that, but what I am trying to highlight is the power of 'balance between effort and surrender' - sometimes, when I read what I write, I wonder if it's me who has written this.

This is what being fascinated with oneself feels like, when you learn to balance the effort with surrender.

~ ~ MY MERAKI NOTES ~ ~

5. Marry the Moment.

I read this tweet somewhere,

If your path is clear, you are not on the right path.

And I was like, what rubbish! Then I was like, maybe it makes sense. Then I was like, but it can't be 100 percent true, or 100 percent false I mean you need to have some clarity at least - the least being - you are unclear about certain things and that you are seeking clarity.

And then I read one more tweet,

It took me years to play like myself.

And then, it made a little more sense what the first tweet implied.

How often do we base our decisions from a place of confusion or fear or unawareness? I have done that for a long time. Most of it was from a place of fear due to confusion and lack of awareness.

What scares you the most?

Let's say you have an exam.

Your fear will be rooted from a place of lack of awareness (you have not studied, clearly you are scared that you will flunk)

Or

From a place of anxiety (you have studied but you are not confident, you are scared you will underperform)

Or

From a place of confusion (you have studied, you always do, you don't score as much as you expect while your friend who doesn't study as much always ends up scoring more than you)

Makes me want to ask you yet another question. Some of you might have the answer at the tip of their tongue while some may take time to arrive at this. Either way, don't think of this as a competition, allow the answer to come to you and keep asking yourself the same question, till you get to the bottom of it.

What is the worst thing you have done because you based a decision from a place of fear?

Whatever your answer is – most of the time – we make no-so-right decisions because we don't play ourselves, we are scared to play ourselves – because we let fear make that decision for us, instead of letting awareness make that decision for us.

The decision we make from a place of self-awareness, by being our own self may seem wrong in that moment from the lens of 'what is supposed to be right' but deep inside a voice will always tell you, that you can make that decision right, go for it – but – you don't listen to that teeny weeny voice and it gets muffled under the loud blaring noises of 'others' of what is 'safe and conventional.' Remember our Shivaji-example.

What do I really mean by – you can make that decision right – because no decision is wrong or right in itself – what may seem like 'the right decision' can go utterly wrong in future, what may seem like 'the wrong decision' could shape up to be the best one you've ever made in life!

~s~c~m~

When it comes to making a decision, we are constantly in a situation of ifs and buts. So, the only way you can make a decision that helps you is when you make it from a place of self-awareness.

When you weight the pros and cons, when you have all the information you need (in that moment), when you know and understand than any decision you make will have consequences – sometimes good, sometimes bad, some in your control, some not in your control.

During the lockdown days, I used to conduct online workshops on 'decision making.'

Would love to share some of my experiences with you, but before that, here's what I want you to do –

So far while reading all these pages, I am sure you have traveled to and fro from your past to future from feeling guilty, regretful to feeling motivated and inspired. Your train of thoughts also halted and paused at stations where you felt sad or disappointed remembering how someone judged you, said or did mean things to you, mocked you.

You've probably also felt burdened with expectations or liberated with acceptance.

You basically had an emotional, overwhelming rollercoaster ride.

So, before you proceed with the next half of the book, take a moment, just look around, look within, do some deep breathing, feel grateful for your blessings, close your eyes, smile, open your eyes, smile broader and hug yourself. Do this, no one is watching you. And if you are in a public place when you are reading this, do it from the comfort of your home, but do this, don't skip.

You have survived this far. I don't mean to undermine real world problems, but problems like these do exist too – problems like feeling lonely, depressed, demotivated, stuck!

And if you have been waiting for a lifeline to be thrown at you because you have felt stuck – this is that lifeline. Take it. You are reading this right now because,

IT IS YOUR TIME.

Timing is the only thing next to Godliness.

And believe me, THIS is that time, YOUR TIME.

So, here's my ask for the next few minutes.

Forget everything – who you are (girl, boy, man, woman, husband, wife, brother, sister, teacher, trader, marketer, dancer, mother, father, actor, writer, researcher, student etc etc). Free yourself from all the multiple roles you have been living for few a minutes. Just be a child – free, open, curious, joyful, playful, restless.

Now, imagine you have a huge, neatly packed gift box, right in front of you.

Excited to open it? Why do we all love gifts, surprises – whether we are a child or an adult?

It's because a surprise comes bearing a certain amount of uncertainty with it. Will it be a surprise if you knew what was inside the box? Will you be as excited as you are now not-knowing what is inside the box vs knowing exactly what is there inside the box – and that's precisely why we call PRESENT a gift. Because, it's like a live game of cricket – where every ball matters – where all you care is playing the game, being in the game – with all the anxiety, excitement of what will happen in the next ball.

We enjoy a live match more than a recorded match whose outcome we already know, right?

That's exactly what I mean by 'marry the moment.'

Going back to 'our gift box' – there's also an element that – the gift box may contain an actual gift or something like a jumping clown that may scare you. So, basically, there's a 50:50 chance of something good or something not so good. In a way you can say that when someone gives you a surprise gift – you want to be 'certain' it's a good-surprise and at the same time you want a certain element of 'uncertainty' so that the surprise-element doesn't lose its essence.

**A good decision is precisely this –
balance between certainty and uncertainty.**

Today, if I were to reveal that 2 years from now, you will be promoted to so-and-so position, 5 years from now you will own a 3bhk in South Bombay, 7 years from now you will be the most successful neurosurgeon in the country etc. etc. will it be any fun in comparison to finding your own path, carving your own niche.

The certainty and uncertainty that comes with every decision you make, is what makes the decision worthwhile.

Today, when I have decided to write this with the aim of reaching out to you, to millions like you, to try to make a difference, to make this a best-seller – can I say with 100% certainty that this will happen – I only have a 50% chance of this happening and I play my bet on this 50% with all of my being, with 100% of my energy, with 100% right intentions in my heart and taking effort in as genuine as possible manner.

I also could have focused on the other 50% - the uncertain 50% and worried about what if things didn't work out – what if I waste a year – what if this, what if that;
but instead I chose to focus on the 50% that excites me, that makes me happy, that gives me sleepless night. It's not easy to simply chuck away a well-paying job, to temporarily settle at an earning 1/5th of what I was making, with the odd freelancing jobs I am currently doing – but I would rather do this NOW than never do it and regret it few years later – regret because I never tried.

All I am saying is – I made a decision fully aware of the pros and cons, I made a decision from a place of self-awareness and by God's grace with my family's support. I also want to reiterate that, I am choosing my struggle, because nothing is easy. And it's a privilege, to be able to choose your struggle.

So don't wait for a 31st December to make your resolutions and goals only to remake it again the next year; decide NOW, act NOW – because if you are reading this, it's a sign. Follow it. Embrace it with both arms.

If ever you want to have a one-to-one conversation about decision-making drop a DM on Instagram at themerakiwoman. Well, the reason I say so is, some decisions can be based on logic, some can't, some decisions are life-altering, some aren't and sometimes a conversation can take your closer in making that decision – with logic, with intuition, gut, with all your being.

~s~c~m~

I read about this amazing concept about **self-awareness being like an onion** in Mark Mason's book, The Subtle Art of not Giving a Fuck.

Stating below the steps which is my interpretation and understanding of Manson's concept:

Step 1: Identify the emotion (I feel sad/happy/uncomfortable/scared/guilty/regretful etc.)

Step 2: Ask yourself why you feel so, what triggered the emotion (This is what made me sad or happy or whatever)

Step 3: Ask yourself why you felt what you felt. Keep digging deeper with why

Everything we feel or think is connected with what we value as an individual. You felt sad because you lost your favorite earring because the value associated with it was that of your boyfriend gifting it to you.

You felt uncomfortable at the thought of meeting new people in new office because you don't like to be superficial, because you are trying to avoid attachment because in your previous office someone hurt you – you can keep diving deeper into the many whys and thus uncover within yourself, the layers of self-awareness.

Something happened in office the other day when I was reading about this and I thought of applying it.

Why do I feel out of place? It is because I am not able to contribute to the conversations.

Why did I feel stupid the moment the question I asked was answered? Is it because it really was a dumb question and I would have easily thought through it by myself, or because what I asked was more like a junior executive level while I had joined there as a senior executive? And let's say, that piece of information slipped my mind and I asked a query (I mean, it's always better to ask than assume)

Why did that one episode jeopardize my entire day. I kept feeling stupid the entire day. I did other things throughout the day, some I outdid myself, some I couldn't do properly simply because the shadow of the morning episode, of me feeling small, kept haunting me.

Why did this teeny-weeny episode have the power to spoil my entire day? I kept asking myself more whys.

I figured that, when I was taking brief from a client, I was sort of trying to show off and then some Energy taught me a lesson by making me feel small. I have spoken about this in one of the earlier chapters how I have sort of always suffered from either of these two complexes - superiority and inferiority.

That incident told me what I valued more - I probably valued self-image over actual learning.

I probably valued short term fixes, salvaging the situation quickly vs actually taking time to understand and offer long term solutions.

I probably always valued short term gratification over delayed but qualitative gratification. Short term gratification isn't always about counting the likes to a post on social media, STG has various forms. I have had a protected childhood, where I was loved and cared and appreciated, so social media likes weren't my blind spot - but the pampering sort of made me feel superior to others than what I really was (than my authentic self) and that bubble had to break someday, eventually making me question my own self-image and then slipping into the inferiority zone for the rest of the day because I felt too ashamed, again feeling ashamed is related to self-image and self-esteem. My self-esteem had always been low and hence it gave the power to petty things, to rule over me, to get my attention for wrong reasons.

The next time you are emotionally charged, emotionally high, go for the onion-layer-test. You will be surprised at your finding.

~s~c~m~

Right now, it feels like I have reached a place where breakthrough success or mediocre success both will mean the same to me, both will get the same neutral reaction/treatment from me. Because, I have realized that I was doing something very important, absolutely wrong all my life. I have over-thought life and people who give a shit or people who are way too casual are far far more successful than I am right now.

Why are some people born with the extra appendages called emotions, like vacuums all over instead of pores on the skin, sucking in, soaking in, way too many emotions than that are needed and can be handled in one lifetime. Why didn't everybody evolve leaving this tail of nasty emotions behind, relying only on logic, if not only, mainly on logic.

On one side we are taught kindness which is a property of the heart, emotions and on the other side, enlightened people on the spiritual path talk more about healthy dissociation from any kind of emotion.

Well, this may seem off-track from the topic of this chapter 'marry the moment' but it isn't.

I have been an overtly emotional and sensitive person all my life. But when you start living in the moment, you automatically stop carry-forwarding the good/bad of the past moment to the present moment and from present moment to future moment.

As cliché as it may sound, meditation helps to arrive and thrive in this 'healthy detachment zone.'

Technique: Just sit by yourself like Sadhguru says and make every thought a third person and just observe it come and go. Google Playstore has an amazing app called Headspace, it's the best guided meditation app I have come across.

I have attended few live workshops of motivational coaches like Sneh Desai, Sandeep Maheshwari etc. Sneh Desai says that the meditation mantra for 'thoughts coming in and going out' is – **from many to one; from one to none.** On day one of your meditation one can't aim for a thought-less state; so one must ensure that it is driven by realistic meditation-goals, broken into smaller goals.

Meaning, on day one start with 5 minutes of sitting in one place and gradually keep adding more minutes per day. Eventually a day will come when the thoughts will have narrowed down from many to one to none. And that could take anywhere from months to years; because meditation involves a great deal of discipline – it's can't be forced, the more you force it, the harder it will be to come by – so one has to be patient and allow it to flow. Use guided meditation apps in the beginning – Headspace is amazing!

~s~c~m~

Gratitude is the strongest prayer and goes a long way in helping you 'marry the moment'.

All my life, I have cursed myself for being this, misfit, yes, I am not exaggerating, cursed, hated, even hit myself physically. But ever since I have become appreciative of what I have, who I am - I have changed, I have become more welcoming, allowing life to welcome me back.

So much of technology thrives on people's fears and insecurities. Had we been comfortable with what we are, we wouldn't have used filters.

But that's not even the bad part. The sad part is, we get very comfortable with what we are, the non-authentic version. It's so much easier to allow filters to invade our life, than to be real.

And real isn't always rude. And technically, real isn't even a version like truth but again what's real for me can be real only in my head, not in reality!

Well, the first place where it happens is your head, your mind creates reality first. Reality for you. And it's not without the deep psychological influences you have absorbed as a child.

Like Dumbledore says, "Of course it is happening inside your head Harry, but why on Earth should that mean it is not real?"

Real is what you make, reality is what others see you have made. Go for it, but first, marry the moment, the only real thing that can help you create your reality.

~s~c~m~

Sharing a few steps that have sort of helped me manage my emotions and marry the moment:

There are so many things that we do knowingly or unknowingly that are constantly leaving impressions on our subconscious.

We often go to bed - angry at someone, irritated with something, disappointed with yourself, unaware of the fact that, while we are fast asleep these unprocessed emotions, thoughts are accumulating in our subconscious – the consequences of which are often unhealthy for the mind.

Following are the steps to befriend your subconscious, the powerhouse of potential, using affirmations. While affirmations are useful, the timing of the affirmation is what will make the real difference.

FIRST STEP

- Don't start affirming right away. Yes, you heard me right. While affirmations are a powerful tool, it's effectiveness depends on how you use it.

- Here's what you need to do: (Let's say the emotion we are dealing with is anger) Accept your anger, to begin with. Tell yourself that you are not angry at yourself or anything, you are probably frustrated with the situation. Acceptance leads to awareness.

- Tell yourself – it's okay to be angry for a while but it's not okay to stay angry because it's not the solution to the problem.

- Give your mind a choice (we are all spoilt for choices) - is staying angry going to help me or hurt me?

SECOND STEP

- Untrained mind is like a monkey jumping on the branches – you have to offer the monkey a banana to prevent itself from jumping aimlessly

- Energy flows where focus goes – divert the anger, channelize the anger. If I tell you don't think of a white elephant, that's exactly what you are going to think about. So, shift focus

- Affirm yourself this: I maybe angry but I am not going to lash out anyone, I will channelize the anger, convert it to something meaningful.

THIRD STEP

- Identify the trigger for that emotion.
- Identify it to un-identify it. Create a space between yourself and the trigger. The emotion that gets triggered by the trigger is not you. You are not the emotion, you are not the thought, you are not the body, you are simply energy.
- There are lot of things that can get you walking on eggshells; waking up to find no milk to make your chai/coffee, seeing someone's post/story on Instagram and comparing yourself, someone saying something or someone not saying something can upset you, getting cranky when hungry; the trigger can be anything and it needs to be identified.
- Make a conscious list of the triggers and create space between the trigger, the emotion and you. This is not easy; it will take practice on a regular basis. You will not even get it right the first time; but you need to keep going.

SUMMARY

- Accept the emotion; don't suppress it.
- Because every time you suppress it, it will find a way to express itself through some other trigger. Accept, acknowledge, let it go.

~s~c~m~

Here's a little exercise, to be a little more aware of your emotions.

1. Things people perceive about me (emotional, cold, sensitive, insensitive, egoistic etc.)

   ____

   ____

2. Things I know about myself (emotional, cold, sensitive, insensitive, egoistic etc.)

   ____

   ____

Check out, how many match; how many don't.

Sometimes our opinions about us can be entirely different from people's perceptions about us – some can be good some can be bad, some can be right some can be wrong.

Don't get overwhelmed and/or carried away by either. Only be aware of what is what. **And work towards marrying the moment.**

~ ~ MY MERAKI NOTES ~ ~

6. Labels or Experience

I have been quite a rebel in my own little way ever since I was a child. I would not agree to everything that my parents would tell me under the tag of 'kids are supposed to do this, only adults get to do that, so on.'

One more thing I have explicitly struggled with is my 'relationship with God.'

For some reason, I always had an understanding of God being Energy and I couldn't fathom the fact that it was split into little units of energy in the form of the dozen idols every Indian household has in their *devhara* (home-mandir-where all the deities are placed and worshiped) And this was one debate my mother and I always would get into, so much that it had led her to believe that I was an atheist because somehow my tender age could not express to her that I believed in the idea of Oneness.

I did a lot of reading, listened to a lot of podcasts, especially for this topic and this is what I have understood.

The many idols in Hinduism doesn't mean 'split energies' as per my assumption – rather it means, there is 'freedom' to choose any 'expression' for worship – it could be an Elephant-Headed god or it could be a tattered clothed Sai Baba – they are not 'split-energies' but representatives of 'ONE' energy and the presence of 33 crore deities only means 33 crore ways in which you can express love and devotion to the One Energy.

By now we know that everything is a 'vibration' and all the mantras and *shlokas* in our culture are different vibrations meant to activate a certain core strength within us. For example – Ganpati is said to be the God of Wisdom, so narration of Ganesh-Mantra and the vibrations of it will in some way activate that part of your brain that helps in memory.

The reason I am stating this is, it makes me feel bad that instead of uniting over this 'experience called energy' we (the humans) are all 'fighting over labels.' We keep going back to what went wrong but not to learn from it, instead use it as victim cards. I really want to urge the youth of our country, supposedly the youngest country comprising 50% population below the age group of 30, to have the right belief systems in place because we are the representatives of our nation, going forward.

~s~c~m~

I want to narrate a small instance from my childhood.

I belong to a Maharashtrian Brahmin Family. Our history textbooks have taught us about the caste system and you will find it hard to believe that until this particular episode happened, I was clueless about what this casteism meant!

And although this happened about almost two decades back, it is still super fresh in my memory.

Here goes, what happened.

After school, like any other day, I was getting ready to go out and play after finishing my glass of milk. I went up and rang Swati's door-bell to ask her if she too was planning to come. Her mother opens the door and says, "Beta, give her 10 min to finish this homework. Then she will come and play with you."

Me: "Okay Aunty. Then I will go ahead, we are playing on the terrace today."

Aunty: "Wait for 10 min na, she's almost done. Take her along. Sit, have some biscuits."

I sit there, on the couch. Munching on to the orange-vanilla-cream biscuit, watching her mother scold her to finish the homework sooner, the motherly way.

Her mother is reading aloud a chapter and teaching her daughter this, "Swati beta, we have faced extreme hardships once upon a time." I am oblivious to what she is saying or about to say, mindlessly swinging my legs, thinking whether or not I should have one more biscuit.

Maybe Aunty realized my hesitation for the biscuit and prompted, "Have na one more." And this time, she goes louder, "So, as I was saying, Swati beta, people of our community had to face a lot of hardships due to the Brahmins, they have ill-treated us for long."

I am still unable to gauge her intention or direction of hurt. But I sense Swati's questioning eyes on me. I thought, maybe I finished the last of her favorite biscuit and as a reflex offer her the biscuit with a slight nod of my head 'do you want it.'

And my innocent trance is broken by her mother asking me, "You are a Brahmin na Ketaki. People of your caste have done atrocities on us. You must be aware of it na. Teach something to her na, she always scores so low in history."

To be honest, I sensed something amiss but really couldn't pinpoint what just happened in there. Before I could make meaning out of 'caste-based atrocities', other building-friends came looking for me. And I ran along with them, with a weird association of never eating those orange-vanilla biscuits ever again.

Many months later when my mother got those orange-vanilla biscuits, that memory sprung up and tears welled up in my out. It reminded me of that silent-taunt – the meaning of which I didn't even fully understand. I told my mother what happened.

This is what my mother had to say to me. "Don't believe what everyone says unless you experience it. Only make experience your teacher, not hearsay. Because everyone's experience of the same situation can be different. Historically speaking, Aunty could be right, but, times change, people learn. And most importantly, we should be the first to learn and change for better. Always prioritize to be a better human first, rest everything, will fall in place." She concluded with a warm hug.

What she didn't add but surely meant must be, 'times change, some people learn, some don't and continue breeding seeds of differences into innocent minds.'

Now when I look back, I realize my obsession with 'experiencism' dates back to that half-formed-understanding of the full-formed-memory.

~s~c~m~

We have had lot of thought-provoking conversations so far. Let me just share a random write-up with you guys, which is more like a short story. The reason being, following the Pomodoro-technique helps; well, this isn't exactly the 25 minutes work 5 minutes break; it's just a little diversion for the mind. So, here goes!

Title: Howzat

The last time I was a cricket fan was way back when I was in 10th standard, that must be more than a decade back.

I had my science II paper, of final board exam the next day and it was an India Pakistan match; I was up till 2 am, cheering and hooting. This guy who was a few years younger to me and stayed a floor below me always responded to my cheering and howzats! We all called him, Amu.

My mother, an extra-proud SBI employee, who had taken

like a month's leave for my exams, majorly supported my hooting with minor bickering in between - it's your boards tomorrow. She knew how much pushing would coax me to study and how much pushing would make me a rebel and give her a push-back. She also knew that if I said, I was prepared, I was prepared. At this juncture of my prepared-ness, forcing me to study would be like feeding a child who is full and making him vomit with just one extra morsel. I knew she wouldn't risk that, after all I had learnt to manipulate from Her Highness only. The way she manipulated His Royalty, my father. The meekest man I ever knew.

Well, that is that, a family of three with Amu downstairs who sort of had feelings for me, because back then I was the only girl in the building who ever watched cricket, didn't bother to bathe on Sundays, didn't bother wearing matching tops and pants, would wipe the sweat on my forehead on the sleeves on my extra-sized T-shirt, would hardly bother to comb my hair even sneak out and apply my father's Old spice after-shave cologne on my clothes (yes clothes, because obviously I didn't have a beard). Not to mention those were the days when Britannia had launched this marketing campaign of having some points on every product and in exchange of those points, World Cup goodies could be received. I was a trader, I always happened to have the exact match of points for the exact item I needed. I may be a manipulator but I was also a kind person. I liked Amu too and I often slipped some of the wrappers with a good number of points into his pocket, bag, books, whatever I could get hold of so that even he ended up getting all the good World Cup merchandise.

But, here's the problem, my liking was restricted to that. I liked him because he was a kind person, he fed stray dogs, was gentle with butterflies, never plucked flowers and buds, even had sort of a pet crow, not like pet as such, but Amu always kept water in small half broken toys, neatly fitted in window gaps for birds and a crow was a regular visitor. I liked him for his kindness.

For some reason, my parents and his parents always got along well. The funny part is, they made us celebrate Raksha-Bandhan as if Amu and I were meant to be some long-lost siblings.

We followed the tradition whether we liked it or not because it always involved small return gifts, until one day, teary eyed Amu came to me with this.

"I don't want to do this anymore, let's just tell them."

I almost burst out laughing looking at his red nose and pearls trickling down from his eyes. "I mean, ya of course, sure, whatever, I am glad you too find this weird."

See, now the thing is, this silly culture of rakhi-brother and rakhi-sister was introduced by parents to the 90's kids back then, purely out of fear. This baby-boomer generation of parents whose sole interest was to provide for their kids, give them best of everything that their parents couldn't give them and strive for our dreams, was scared that their pure interests were at risk if ravaging hormones were not rakhi-bound.

“Let’s go tell them.” I insist to Amu before his tears and determination both dry up.

Amu looks shocked and surprised. “Why don’t you want to continue this rakhi-tradition?”

I simply shrug, with my signature look, do I look like I care. Amu quickly speaks as if he knows that my *I don’t care* could prove dangerous. He says, “I want us to tie another bond. Not the one that you tie on my wrist, but the one I will tie around your neck.”

Thud.

It’s the sound of me slapping him. I don’t know what came over me, I was never a volatile person, because most of the time, my look was enough. But that sentence was the catalyst to my non-volatile-enzyme; the reaction to which was that slap.

“Do you want to make me your pet dog? How sick of you…”

“Noooo…” comes his trembling voice, as his cheeks recover from the reflex of my palm. I meant this…” saying so, he removes a black beaded chain-thing from his pocket.

“Have you totally lost it? From where did you even get that? And how old are you, you are not even…. gosh…” clearly, I was getting hysterical.

***

The only reason I had opted dropping out of the rakhi-tradition was because I genuinely liked Amu and forcing a label for a relation seemed to insult what I felt for him, and what I felt for him wasn't brotherly nor was it boy-friendly, I mean, why can't people ever have relations, wherein they get to like each other without these tags, labels. I find it suffocating and today after all these years, this is the one thing about me that hasn't changed.

What has sadly changed is the way I express it, rather the way I don't express it, the way I have given in to so-called society's ways of living.

Even back then, I loved what I shared with my parents. I mean, one can't change the fact that they are parents, but my mother, knowingly and unknowingly allowed me to be a lot of things to her. Sometimes, I was her fashion critique, when she asked me how she looked, draping a saree and fixing up an attire and damn she took my advice seriously. I was even her advocate when she cribbed about her husband and asked me what I would do if I were in her place. At times, she took me to her office where I got to be around the ladies and felt like an insider to the gossip-party, felt like a friend. With my mother I had this multiple-role playing relationship as a little girl and with my father we were always like those mysterious strange neighbors, who didn't talk on an everyday basis but were always updated about what was happening in each other's lives.

When I went to college, had my first boyfriend and sort of expressed this to him, he kind of got weird as if I was crazy. I mean I told him, "It's good to have you in my life, but can we not call each other GF/BF every time. I mean, that's what we are but sometimes, we can be just friends to one another, sometimes have fist-fights like siblings, sometimes show care like a parent would, by just falling asleep in the lap or cooking a nice meal and of course be lovers, kiss and make out and … you know what I mean."

"I understood what you are proposing because I understand the language but I am pretty sure, this is not what I understand as a feeling and I am surely not in favor of this illogical thing."

No, we didn't break up immediately, this was the Gen Y we are talking about, not today's Gen Z who communicates in GIFs and don't even have formal break-ups - you get ghosted online, consider it a break-up! We went on for almost two years after this conversation but I figured it was what led to that piled up break-up.

Is it wrong to expect this from a relationship? Or is it that my idea of relations or my idea of love is flawed. Not flawed in itself, but maybe so uncommon and unheard of that, against a collective nature of what is accepted, this seems like an unwanted-child, an uninvited guest, an unprocessed entity.

Or is it that, something like this was once upon a time so common in a parallel world somewhere, that eventually someone thought it was boring; boring because it's more peaceful, less dramatic and changed the rules only to add some masala.

I do have a problem with structures. It's like watching a cricket match whose outcome you already know. And I started losing interest in the cricket match, something that was so close to me, after the betting-scam. Sometimes, it takes one truth or one lie to change your lens of everything. The truth, that the matches were fixed. The lies, that the players were not playing their game. When you put a name to a relationship, it's as if there is just one coloured-lens you have to wear all your life, it's as if one lie or one truth you have to live all your life with that person. It's suffocating for me, and me saying this and/or even feeling this is unacceptable in this society.

I have been in enough relationships after that to realize that Murphy was right. What is meant to go wrong will go wrong. But this is not the only thing Murphy is right about. He also says, "the amount of love someone feels for you is inversely proportional to how much you love them."

Love is the most overused but most under-understood word. I can say I loved Amu, but my kind of love for him and his kind of love for me always clashed. And of course, just like I never gave myself a chance to feel that way for him, he never gave a chance to himself to be on the other side of *that feeling* for me. We were too naive to consider the possibility of the other person being right.

Maybe it was the forced Rakhi, or it was the conditioning that a guy can't be younger to the girl or whatever, we drew boundaries in our minds after that day, instead of trying out a power-play we started fielding our emotions so fiercely that we never let a feeling take a full swing sixer.

I don't know where he is today and what he does in life these days. Yes, it's easy to find out things today, and I can, but I won't because this kind of finding is called stalking. This kind of finding is for love that is lost and was waiting to be found. My love for him was never lost, it was always there, it will always be there, but maybe this time, I am willing to express it differently. Maybe this time even he is also willing to receive it differently; the way I give - like a game of cricket - play in the moment, be in the moment - bat, bowl, field, lose, win - it's all part of the game - loving the game is all that matters.

~s~c~m~

Before we move on to the next chapter, I just hope all these conversations have been helping you so far.

Don't be a label, don't stay fixated to one thing, be open, be flexible about possibilities. Don't let bitter experiences with people make you bitter. Don't stop being kind just because someone isn't and at the same time be fierce and protect your kindness. Just like you lift up your friend who is in trouble or bad mood, be that friend for yourself too, be kind to yourself too. Don't let one poor decision hold you back from making the next right decision.

The world has all kinds of people. And mind you, every person who has ever met and will ever meet is for a reason. God never plants anyone in your life randomly. Some are meant to give you those scars – because God wants you to bounce back stronger in life. It's really what you do with those scars – turn them into stepping stones or keep playing victim; the choice is all yours.

Most important of all; spread the word, because you are most likely to attract your kind of people – so, there's a fair chance that the labels you wear are also the labels they wear and if shedding those labels has helped you, it will help them too.

There's this quote by J.Krishnamurthy that has stayed with me;

If you begin to understand what you are without trying to change it, then what you are undergoes a transformation.

In the context of labels and experiences; we first need to learn to see ourselves as is – as is – means – with the flaws with the imperfections - what you are without trying to change it – as an integral part of you. Once you know that, once you are fully aware of that – only then can you undergo unbiased transformation – that aligns with your authentic self.

~ ~ MY MERAKI NOTES ~ ~

7. Lost and Found!

I was badly shaken with a conversation I had with someone close. Shaken because at the surface of denial there was a scary but liberating truth.

And I don't know whether or not it's appropriate to mention this very personal conversation here, but, then what am I doing if I am not writing about my fears, being as real as I can be.

He asks me, "You don't miss me now-a-days like you used to."

I press my eyes, cringe my eyelids, trying to grasp the meaning of those raw words and give him a hug so that he doesn't see my eyes expressing dismay. I am shaken but I don't show him that (that's a rare ability I have which for the longest time I felt was more like weakness than strength, but a friend made me realize it's more of a strength than a weakness, more on this later).

I tell him, more like a plea in my voice than an ask, "What makes you say that? If that had not been the case, I would not have texted you, pointing out that our silences are growing and the distance is hurting."

He agrees verbally with a 'hmmm' but he is not convinced and I know that. He knows that I know it.

Without context this conversation can be dismissed as something you don't want to pay heed to, but given the context, relevance and impact it had on me, I want to elaborate more on this.

I read this in Mark Manson's book 'The Subtle Art of Not Giving a Fcuk'

It's worth remembering that for any change to happen in your life, you must be wrong about something.

If you are sitting there, miserable day after day, then that means you are already wrong about something major in your life and until you are able to question yourself to find it, nothing will change.

Crazy lines, right? So full of deep shit!

It's worth remembering that for any change to happen in your life, you must be wrong about something.

He also told me that there were some major visible changes in me since the past couple of years. Yes, major change had happened within me, since past two years to be precise, because I was grossly wrong about major things in life; the most important being – my relationship with myself.

I was in self-denial, always finding faults with myself, chaotic and confused about what I wanted from life vs what I thought I wanted from life given the influence of my inner circle. I was vulnerable and gave the power of validation to others which led me to making a lot of decisions from a place of non-acceptance of self, from a place of fear-of-rejection.

And the burden of all this, was always expecting things from those few people in my life who are my support system – expecting them to be there for me emotionally, to pick me up when I was low, to push me to do better etc.

All this changed in the last two years; and no it didn't happen overnight, it happened over many nights of making small changes in my life. Trust me I quit every day, just that I kept going. I cried and gave up too, but didn't stay there. I kept building on small habits every day.

I started taking responsibility for myself, for my peace, for my happiness, for my dreams – the focus suddenly shifted from finding pieces of broken-me through others to first accepting the broken-me and being patient about healing myself without hatred, accepting that I will fall and I will be there to pick myself up, because I didn't want to stay fallen, because I was okay to fall as long as I was learning and growing. So suddenly my emotional dependency on close friends, family decreased and I didn't know it was so evident until he pointed it out to me.

And I believe he did that, because there was a time when he was my go-to-person for everything but today I am my go-to-person. **So, yes, in the course of this change, you may find yourself getting distant from the people you love, from the people you were once extremely close to, but if that means, getting closer to finding yourself, getting closer to being yourself, getting closer to feeling whole within without being toxic to your loved ones (like I was once) – I say, go for that change**.

Go for it if you have felt you were wrong about something in life, go for it and give yourself a chance to right the wrong.

In the same chapter, Mark Manson quotes Aristotle, 'It is the mark of a realized mind to be able to entertain a thought without accepting it.'

Trust me there's nothing new I have trying to tell here that someone else hasn't already said, it's just how I share and how you receive that will make your life a *life of meraki.*

I was watching a series on Netflix named, Sweet Magnolias. There's a conversation that goes between two people.

Person 1 is going through a consultation of the sorts, trying to reconcile with her husband because they had

mutually separated for some reason.
Person 2 is giving her the consultation.

Person 1:
"Sometimes I want to forgive and forget and move on, that means letting go off all the anger, all the hurt and maybe if I let off, I will fall apart, because I have been holding on to it so much that – it feels a part of me."

Person 2:
"Let it fall apart because only then, you will be able to build something new."

Sometimes, we hold on to our broken-ness and hurt like a scorpion. Knowingly and unknowingly, they start becoming a part of us, almost like a symbiotic relation. We get so used to it, so comfortable with it that at time when life does offer a chance to forget, forgive and move on, we feel, what will be left of us if we let go of those parts of us – sometimes remaining broken becomes a comfort zone!

~s~c~m~

Now, I have a theory.

Let's say every person is made up of 100 units.

50 units are made up of the everyday things we all do, our basic needs – food, clothing, shelter, education, jobs, careers, vacations, marriage etc.

The other 50 is sort of wild, unprocessed, open ended and comprises of passion, hobbies, various interests – most of which are intangible or won't add up as is – like for example passion for singing, interest in sports, love for travel etc. – the list can be endless.

The thing is most people survive with the first 50 units – for them these 50 units make up the 100 units. Some of them do realize the presence of the other 50 units too and try to keep that aspect of their lives alive.

For some others, the second set of 50 units start occupying more space, more value and they need to keep that part of them more than just alive!

Basically, to keep every unit alive, there has to be a source, something that charges it. For the first 50 it's your family, friends, relatives, peers, colleagues but for the next 50 it has to be someone who resonates with that feeling, only then can you charge the other 50 units of energy.

Otherwise a major part of that person will go uncharged, unhappy. What I mean to say is, once you start identifying your calling – you need to have the right circle of people, you need to have your tribe so that there is a healthy exchange and recharge of every unit of energy.

Just an example to explain this better:

My partner's second set of 50 units comprises numbers, stock markets, businesses etc. I totally can't relate to half of it and we can't really have enriching discussions on those topics. My second set of 50 units comprises words, stories, art etc which he can't entirely relate to. When we talk on these topics it's more about 'sharing information' than about 'enriching discussions.'

Remember, I have mentioned this so many times by now – how he has been my first everything – and that's why unknowingly I burdened him with the responsibility of charging those 50 units for me.

Now, recall that dialogue from Dear Zindagi wherein SRK says, "*...hum apni sare expectations ka bhoj us ek rishte pe dete hai...*"

We shouldn't be doing that. What we should be doing instead is meet different people, take exposure as much as possible – find our tribe and associated with like-minded people.

In the process you may hurt someone close but if there's love and understanding, things will fall in place – not only that, **you will find yourself closer to that one person with whom you the spend majority of time – you, yourself.**

~s~c~m~

Mind, body, soul and energy:

The laws of energy are always working, whether or not you are.

You lose something, you gain something; you gain something you lose something.

We may be making random choices every day and one choice will not initiate this give and take on an immediate basis, it's a series of those choices that will.

But there will come a day when that one choice will make all the difference; because you will have reached your threshold by then.

This will hold true for a good habit and for a bad habit both.

Eating one burger won't affect your health, skipping a workout for one day won't make you gain pounds, the repetitive actions will. Similarly eating your green for one day won't make you healthier nor will going to the gym for one day make you fitter. Telling yourself 'I am stupid' won't make you stupid, or telling yourself 'I am intelligent' won't make you intelligent. **It's always the small things that add up, that compound, that show visible results**.

I had mentioned in the earlier chapters that 2020 was my do or die moment. It's been two years now (it's April 2022) I have been doing few things on a regular basis, with a lot of commitment. And all those small habits have started adding up.

Would like to share the same here:

1. Shambhavi Mahamudra

This is a spiritual process that Sadhguru teaches and it is strictly advised that one must learn this directly from the guru; don't try to learn this from YouTube videos. Check out the induction program on their website www.ishafoundation.com

I have been doing this practice almost everyday now for the past 2 years, first thing in the morning.

How it has helped me? I have been able to make better decisions, from things as simple as – choosing healthy food over junk food to choosing to stay away from toxic people to prioritizing things that matter. Earlier I was quite an indecisive person, but I got better, I started making decisions from a place of awareness.

2. Journaling

I have been journaling all my life but that was just regular rants and complaints about things, and that's what I kept getting back in return. I changed the way I journaled.

It's always better to vent out negative thoughts on a piece of paper than on a person or situation which I also did; but one needs to back up the problem statements with solution-driven statements.

Eg. If I write in my diary that 'I had a bad day at work because of my boss, he said a lot of nasty things to me. I hate him, he's an ***.'

This is accepting the emotion that you are angry and then venting out on a paper; try doing this with pen and paper; without filtering your emotions, let them out.
After all the negative ranting is done, get a closure with a positive statement.

Eg. Ya, I had a bad day at work because I feel my boss was unfair or because my mom-in-law is so bitchy or whatever. But I can't change his or her nature, I can't give him or her the power to upset me. Also, what could I do to perform better at work, do I need to upgrade any skills?

Like we agreed, everything is energy at the end of the day. If we try to suppress what we feel, it will have an outlet somewhere else.

So, it's best to let it flow without hurting anyone, like it usually happens – if I am feeling upset about something, I will be cranky and take it out on my partner or parents – we don't want that. We want a smooth transition from problem to solution. So, venting out on paper helps and once the negative energy is out, there is more space for the positive thoughts for the positive energy, for all the affirmations.

I repeat, doing this activity once will not help you as much as doing it everyday will. **When you repeat it over and over again, you are building up a reserve of**

affirmations in your subconscious there will come a time when – you will automatically respond to a situation in the best possible way. You will not be in the conscious decision-making trap of whether to eat a burger or a banana, you will automatically pick the banana, the healthier option. But this subconscious conditioning will happen when you take small conscious steps every day.

3. Surya Namaskar

I owe this entirely to my mother, the habit of me doing at least 11 rounds of Surya Namaskar right from my childhood. In school days, during summer she would up the number to 20, 30, sometimes 50 and it was an incentive-based exercise for me. Like maybe getting an extra helping of ice-cream!

I continue it to this day, at least 4 to 5 times a week, if not every day.

4. Weight training and Cardio

I added some weights to my daily Surya Namaskar routine and I feel strength along with the flexibility that the Surya Namaskar offered. Of course, it's not a very intensive thing, but, I am doing it in my own way, taking baby steps.

For some reason, my cardio is restricted only to walking, that too only over weekends, that too very irregular. So, ya, that's still a work-in-progress.

5. Meditation and Mantra.

Ranveer Allahbadia had mentioned on one of his podcasts about the positive effects of Hanuman Chalisa on cognition, behavior and action-taking ability. I have always believed in the power of mantras because it's a sound and we know that everything is a vibration. So, it's been some months now, I have included that as a part of my meditation. Letting you in on a secret – at times, I put it on loop and end up writing a mad number of pages

6. Content consumption

Just like you are what you eat, you also are what you consume. I started consuming a lot of motivational content and throughout the book, you have found many references to all the people who have helped me, be this version of me. I am truly grateful for all the content creators out there, who are my gurus, who are gurus to all the people out there, bless them all!

One content-based trivia is that, during the lockdown, I also discovered Suits (the Harvey Specter sitcom), all thanks to my partner. And believe it or not, it helped me improve my logical and reasoning skills. I mean, as far as I know, I haven't been the most logical person! I watch Suits as often as I can, I even have a Suits based poster at my place.

7. 5 am club

Now, this has been a personal high for me, when it comes to a milestone. Because, I have been notoriously famous for being an owl, a late riser, with nasty morning habits. From being that person to slowly changing my body clock to being a 5 am person, I really feel proud of myself.
The first two hours of the morning, before the world wakes up, are a true bliss! All the things I mentioned above, I usually accomplish in the first two hours of the day, 5 am to 7 am. I did this straight for one and half year in 2020 and 2021. I started small, waking up 30 minutes before my usual wake-up, tapering it to finally hitting the 5 am mark!

Again, honest confession, I haven't been doing that for 2 months I have quit the job because I write at erratic hours, sometimes the writing strikes at night, in the morning – so at most times, I end up sleeping at erratic hours, and then waking up at 5 am becomes a task. However, whatever time I wake up, I ensure I start my day with Shambhavi and all the things I have mentioned above – on most days, 4 to 5 times a week and I need to up this number to 6 times a week – working towards it.

So, all in all, this is how I lost a few things, found a few things and it's an ongoing process.

Well, see the thing is what works works,
what works for you may not work for me,
what works for me may not work for you.

For example: If I am writing something, I try to keep myself away from posting anything on Insta/YT because it distracts me, it takes away a part of my energy and then affects my writing. So usually when I am writing, I avoid posting - that's how I function. However, I do want to eventually build my Insta handle and YouTube channel too.

That could be because, as a skillset I am not a very good multitasker, I am more of a one thing at a time person. And in my current choice of career this works in my favor. In my previous career, I didn't have the luxury to not be a multitasker.

So, for somebody else, writing (one interest) and posting on social media (other interest) can work parallel – it could act as a source of motivation, for me it's a source of leak in energy and that's why I refrain from posting.

Be your own person, lose yourself, find yourself;
make your own variations of what works
best for you, what doesn't.

Rules are meant to act as guidelines or templates,
bend them, modify them;
be creative with the rules, too.

~s~c~m~

~ ~ MY MERAKI NOTES ~ ~

8. Are you in a relationship with yourself?

There's this quote by Einstein- If you judge a fish by its ability to climb the tree, it will live its whole life believing that its stupid.

I genuinely believe that we are all unique in our own way and simply aping the herd mentality without giving a chance to discover who you truly are, is equivalent to cheating – it's cheating yourself.

You can make a difference in this world only with what you have, not what your neighbor has.

You might be good at art; your neighbor might be good at math – neither of you is going to be half as good if we take away that aspect from you.

The world needs both, so be yourself, only then can you be happy, only then can you make a positive impact.

I always quote this profound message by Sadhguru, "Consciousness is the basis of creation." You can create anything you want if you start raising the level of your consciousness, if you meet your true self.

I have a small quiz for you.

Imagine there are three pictures in front of you:
tree, tiger, man.

Who is physically stronger? Tiger
Who can live longer? Tree

By their bodily constitution, a tiger will be stronger, a tree will live longer; that's the quality of their life. A man won't stand a chance in comparison to them in these parameters. But man can do other things using the power of consciousness, the power of creation to navigate this way through this, let's say by making tools that can help him be stronger in front of a tiger.

Man is the only animal on this planet with this power. At the same time, man is the only animal on the planet with the ability to make choices.

When a tiger is hungry and a deer runs by him – is he going to tell himself *"Naah, let me eat something else today?"* or will he tell himself, *"Wow, deer is my favorite, let me eat two."* He eats only as per his hunger, goes on to do his daily activities.

Humans are the only ones born with an ability to make a choice, the choice to make the best use of our conscious – the source of creation. This is us, having the creator's gene! And what do we do?

When roti-sabji is offered, we want a burger, when burger is offered, we want biryani and so on. No, I am not saying *'don't eat a burger or biryani'* – what I am mean by 'we do have the ability to make a choice' – of course you should eat burger once in a while – I love vada-pav and I do indulge in having one, even two a times – but when I make that choice – I have ensured that I have balanced by day's diet not just with healthy food but also exercise – moderation is the key.

Commit to yourself. Commit to making the best possible choices for yourself. Commit to being in the best possible relationship with yourself.

They say trust is a two-way street, they say trust is always black and white, it's there or not there and for some reason, I have always lived on the edge.

I never trusted myself.

I have always let my own self down and never had a steady relationship with myself. One day I was this person, other day I was that person.

Every time I felt I was at a rock bottom, I surprised myself with another rock bottom, making and breaking my own benchmarks.

Today when I look back, I know why, I have let people do things to me – manipulate me, be mean to me, rude to me, because a part of me was so neglected by my own self, that I was on a frenzy of validations from people – the kind of people who seemed right, but only right lessons for me.

When I look back at things with today's sense of self-awareness, I don't fool myself into thinking that *'I had no choice.'* I know for a fact that; I could have chosen better things for me. One almost always has a choice.

Relationship with yourself…

1. Starts with Forgiveness.

Forgiving yourself for the things you didn't do, that you always expected from yourself.

Even if you take away this one thing from this entire book, you will have made a positive impact in your life and trust me, that's just the start – slowly and steadily this positive impact on your individual life will reflect in every walk of life – your relation, your loved ones, your relation with health, your relation with money, your relation with success, your relation with creativity, your relation with happiness, your relation with satisfaction, your relation with kindness, your relation with growth, your relation with receiving well, your relation with giving back, your relation with peace.

Forgive that inner child who carried forward the hurt, unknowingly, who sought your attention by doing rebellious self-sabotaging things.

Embrace him/her unconditionally. When you forgive yourself, you will upgrade to a place of forgiving other people who you think/feel have hurt you – remind yourself, even they have an inner child who has been hurt – they didn't pass on the hurt on purpose, they did it because they were holding grudges too – with themselves, with other people in their life.

Relationship with yourself…

2. Builds with Gratitude.

Lockdown has made many of us realize what 'gratitude' is. It's this one thing, that is hands down directly proportional to who you turn out to be – bitter or better.

I mean, every other thing I have mentioned so far can have varying intensities depending on who is reading, how it's being understood and received, how it's being applied – it could be subject to individual interpretations to an extent. But gratitude is the constant to these variables.

The more grateful you are about what you have, the more of it you will have.

And I am not asking you to 'visualize' about being grateful. The way visualization works is, let's say you have aimed for a brand-new car – you imagine with your thought and feeling that you have the car already. The Secret by Rhonda Byrne explains this in detail. It's available as a book and movie. Go check it out.

That's not how gratitude works at the fundamental level. At the core of it, gratitude means – feeling thankful for the car that you currently have – feeling it with all the genuineness you can possibly muster – thinking about all the amazing moments you could experience because of that car, only because of that car – being thankful that maybe if it wasn't for that car – your dog could not have survived that accident or you wouldn't have bonded with that person in your life who was once your friend but is now your life partner, it was all because conversations you had over the long-drives etc.

The way gratitude functions is letting the Universe, the Force, Whoever you have fully surrendered to, know how much you appreciate what you have in the moment because there could be so many who dream of having what you have – the health you have, the parents you have, the job you have, the friends you have, that gift of painting/singing that you have, that latest i-phone you so casually own, that movie date you have, the clean water you use so casually, the tiffin your mom packs for you, the first mango of the season your father gets for you, the loved one at home who waits for you, the cooling-effect of

AC you sleep off too – don't you think, all these should be your last thoughts and feelings for the day when you hit of in the cozy bed with air-conditioning – wouldn't it be nice to be thankful instead of cribbing about what you don't have 'yet.'

I don't know if this sounds 'too much' but I have also realized that, every time you get what you wanted – that 'getting' moment is temporary – it's fleeting.

What will stay with you even after that moment is 'how you reached there.'

Were you grateful for all those who contributed to your 'getting' there? Did you thoroughly 'enjoy' the process of 'getting' there? Are you happy with the kind of person you have become.

If you have answered YES to all these, you will have *meraki in your life*, every moment; not only that, you will be a powerhouse of *meraki* for everyone around you. You will glow differently.

I will share a personal example with you.

I am not very good at receiving compliments. I never considered myself beautiful. When people complimented the way I smiled or dressed or looked, I would kind of be casual about it, not really rude, but it would be like 'ya okay, big deal, there are prettier people than me.' For me, I would have been happier, had they appreciated me for being smart or brainy or aced at mathematics because I was pathetic with numbers and I was always fascinated with people who were good at it.

It took a really bad hospitalization for me to value what I had. It took a very bad toll on my health; post-recovery phase was also very slow - all the external features were like good skin, good hair, nice smile etc. were literally starting to look scary because I had lost weight, there were post-operative scars at many places on my body, my eyes looked empty, I was losing my hair the way a chemo-patient does, I had to get a supremely small boy-cut, like the military people do it. I could not walk without support.

All the comments I used to receive were suddenly changing into ones filled with pity, with get well soon wishes. I could not look at myself in the mirror. I regretted postponing participating in marathons, because I wondered if I could even walk normally. I never cried in front of my parents, but I would often cry myself to sleep because I looked so scary and wondered if I would ever be normal again!

It was only because of my family's love and support that I eventually recovered. And it was after that incident I started appreciating the gifts, the blessings of health and beauty and kindness! I feel extremely embarrassed to share that, I have done that to 'my writing' too – forget being appreciative, I have cursed it, because there are times in my writing-phase when I am not-myself, and it has affected my loved ones.

But the day I changed this equation with 'my writing' things started falling in place, and of course it's always an ongoing process, being better, every day, taking one day at a time.

Relationship with yourself…

3. Grows with Faith.

Do you know about the Fern and Bamboo story?

One day, a man got very frustrated with his life. He was at a stage where he felt, nothing was working in his favor, he was demotivated that all his efforts were met with dead ends. He wanted to give up, that's when he happened to meet GOD.

He opened his complaint box to God; God listened to him, smiled at him and then started narrating a story.

"You know that, things happen when they are meant to, don't you? Everyone has a timing, every living being on this Earth is different, has a different purpose to achieve and based on the purpose, the timing differs."

"How so?" The man asks.

"All my kids are equal for me, be it a man or a plant or an animal. When I plant a Fern seed, it starts flowering within weeks but when I plant a Bamboo seed, do you how know much time it takes?"

"Few months, maybe." The man shrugs.

"5 years!"

"Whaaat!" The man can't believe it!

"By that logic, I should be angry at the Bamboo seed, right? But I am obviously not, because the seed took 5 years to build a strong root network underground, so that in a few months it could grow into a 60-foot tree!"

"Hmmm." The man utters.

"What you see outward is not always what's happening on the inside. You may feel, I don't see your efforts, but you may not know what plans I have for you. Also, you need to stop comparing yourself with others. Everyone is different. Everyone's karma is different. Just like the Bamboo seed, you should keep growing within, upgrading life skills and **most importantly belief in yourself, because no one will, if you don't**."

Sometimes, if life, we do feel demotivated, we feel 'why aren't the wheels of time' shifting in my favor, when I am taking the effort. We probably give up at a point where we are just about to cross that 'plateau of latent potential' and achieve something remarkable. And when we give up at this point, we have to kind of start all over again.

I read about the 'plateau of latent potential' in James Clear's book, Atomic Habits.

He explains it with a very simple and effective example.

Let's say you have some ice cubes in front of you and the temperature is around 25 degrees F. Your aim is to melt the ice. You start taking effort (increase the temperature by one degree, 26, 27, 28 you go on, you push yourself for 29, 30, 31 even if you are tired; but somehow give up at 31 and had you pushed a little more, showed a little more faith in your effort, you would have hit 32, the ice would have started melting!

~s~c~m~

I am a huge huge huge believer in universal signs! I want to mention the latest one I got in the context of this book. I had been to an exhibition with my mother, there were all kinds of things there – paintings, bags, jewelry etc. The main reason we opted to go there was to sort of show our support, to encourage one of our relatives who had put up a stall there – hers was the one with paintings.

We bought a few things and then we were chatting with her. We did a few rounds of the exhibition and ended up buying a few more things too. We then came up to her to say 'good-bye' before we left from there; and you know what she gave me?

A bookmark that said, 'just one more chapter.'

And that was exactly where I was placed in terms of this book – this last chapter was in the making! My eyes got a little moist and I told her - there can't be a bigger sign than this. Because, I am not really the 'attending the exhibition' kind. I just happened to say 'yes' when mother asked me if I wanted to tag along with her.

Believe me the Universe is always speaking to you, always showing you – once you know how to listen to what it's saying, how to see what it's showing you – some things just opens up magically – the possibilities start showing itself like a catalog – all you have to do it put your finger on it and add to your cart – work towards it, and it's yours.

However, making 'something' yours and being 'someone' who has 'that something' are slightly two different things. When your end goal is 'something' you associate your identity with 'something'; when your end goal is 'being someone' that becomes your identity.

Example: End goal is losing 10 kg vs End goal is being healthy.

Depending on what your end goal is, you are constantly engaged in a dialogue with your mind. When your end goal is 'being healthy' you will automatically make better choices – eat healthy, hit the gym, meditate, read and be in the company of like-minded people. It may look like a small thing – but it makes a lot of difference when you focus on 'who' you want to be vs 'what' you want to be.

This is how I try to apply this.

What I want to do is – write 10 pages a day
Who I want to be is – a writer

Writing 10 pages a day is surely a good discipline to have, but I will be subjected to 'good days' and 'bad days' – I will have to push myself.

But when I tell myself – I am a writer, I want to be a better writer each day – I will do whatever it takes to be that – meaning – along with subjecting myself to the discipline of writing 10 page/day, I will also read a lot, I will take healthy writing breaks, I will take care of my posture, I will see to it I do everything it takes to be that person, I will inculcate within me, every other discipline that will compound in making me a better writer.

I read about this in Atomic Habits – every small step you take is like building a unit of evidence towards who you are becoming.

And the reverse is equally true.

When you give up on the ice cubes at 30-degree F or 31-degree F, the evidence you are building for yourself is 'you can't finish a task' or 'you don't have it in you.' Next time you take up a task, this is the evidence that will show up first. Eventually that will be your 'identity,'

Your identity-system will be like – 'I don't trust this person (you) to do this', 'He will screw up again.', 'She's a quitter.'

Your identity-system will tell you – you are an unhealthy person, you are not a writer, so on and so forth – and needless to say, what your choices will be like.

So, build pockets of proof for yourself.

It's every small win that counts,
that adds up as evidence.

It's like a muscle –
the more you do it,
the more you have it,
the more you have it,
the more it becomes ingrained in your system
and becomes a part of your identity,
becomes a part of you – becomes you.

Eventually it leads you to making lesser decisions – about making a choice; because you will end up making a better choice as a pattern.

That eventually gives your mind more space, more energy to do the things that you are meant to do; that move you closer to your purpose, your authentic self – towards what you are meant to be.

Go claim it! It's yours already.

Ankur Warikoo says in Do Epic Shit, **'document your journey.'**

When I read about it, I DMed him on Instagram about how it motivated me to continue writing Second Chance to Meraki; the book was more than half done by then, but somehow, the pace had slowed down – he helped me pick up pace. And he has always been kind enough to reply back to all my DMs. I really owe it to him and everyone else out there, who's references I have used here, because they have all left huge impressions on me and contributed in making me whoever I am shaping to be and I want it to be a continuous process.

I never want to hit 100% about this, I want to be at 99% because there will always be a scope to be better, isn't it?

Well, by documenting my journey, I am building proof my myself, for my identity-system, that I can be who I want to be, every day.

~s~c~m~

Languages and how they have evolved have always fascinated me and here's an example of how they are deeply rooted with our evolution.

The other day I was having a conversation with a cousin and she said something about 'give and take.'

Sometime later it got me thinking, how in almost every language, it's 'give' first and 'take' later – as a usage.

In Hindi, we say, '*ek haat se do, dusre haat se lo.*' In Marathi there's a term '*devan-ghevan.*' Try applying this in your own respective language. The point is – you have to 'give' first in order to 'receive', what you 'give' is what you 'get.'

You have to 'give' the necessary time to 'get' what you want, to become who you want to become.

Sadhguru has said this in many of his videos – commit to just one thing in life – be it anything – and see where life takes you.

Every decision you make, will then be in alignment with that commitment, will help in building the identity-proof we spoke of.

If I am committed to being a writer, every decision will be a fall out of that. If I have committed to completing this book within a deadline – then, I will have to drop out of that party or the family gathering or that IPL match – if it is going to come in the way of my deadline and commitment.

But if I am stuck in my writing and I feel that party will help me get back on track, then I can attend it for some time and come back and finish the number of pages I have decided to complete.

Saying No to that party might hurt your friends, but if they are your friends they will understand. You live up to your commitment first, keep the promise you made to yourself, give what it takes and then party harder. **Get your priorities straight.** You can't please everyone. Someone once told me, **focus is sacrifice.**

There are many of us who may not believe in God or a Force beyond us. But let me ask you something – didn't we learn mathematical hypotheses in school?

Didn't we first assume something exists (like A = B) and then proved it eventually. Can't we assume this about the Bigger Force too, believe that, IT always wants what is best for us.

Even if there are struggles, pitfalls, they are meant as stepping stones. **Belief is magical. The more you have it, the more it works for you.** It's not the reverse – you can't say – let IT work for me, then I will believe in it. It's like saying – *I can't run because I am fat, let the fat go, then I will start running.* That's not how the law of give-take works. You need to start running first, then there is every possibility that the extra fat will turn into healthy-fat.

The only sure shot way to better your relationship with yourself is to constantly believe in who you want to be, and then start working towards it.

~s~c~m~

There's one thing I am still trying to understand as a life lesson is what's the exact point when one should start standing up for oneself because I feel there's a very minute difference between healthy ego (self-respect) and unhealthy ego.

I mean, 9 out of 10 times, I have always 'reacted' to a situation when it's late, when it's at the tipping point – be it some misbehaving or saying or doing something inappropriate with me, be it a colleague manipulating me or putting me down in front of a superior, be it being on the hearing side for no fault of mine. I mean, one may allow this once or twice out of trying to be the bigger person or trying to be understanding but every time is a little unbelievable, isn't it?

Sometimes what I have understood as being-tolerant has almost every time turned against me and it made me realize (not really act upon it in the fullest sense yet) that people are who they are. They are passing down what they have been receiving. And while most times, I have stayed silent and taken on the insults because I have always been of the 'let it go' types.

I simply can't tolerate conflicts for some reason and
have given in to the demanding person or given in to the situation without a fight because, I have always felt that 'maybe, if I am considerate this one time he/she will let it pass, maybe he/she is venting out of hurt, I have always told myself *'jaane do na'*, let me work on myself, see how I can be better.

Almost at every farewell at every place I have worked with, my colleagues have told me this one thing, almost every time – 'you don't know to quantify things, you don't know how to put up your work up there' and every time I decide I will act upon this in the next organization I end up not doing it as much as needed.

See, it's a disaster for me to say this in this cut throat competitive corporate world, but deep down I have always believed that – if someone doesn't 'see' the value you have been offering, then either you aren't offering it or that person will never see – and if someone has to 'see' that value, then he/she will see it irrespective of whatever.

By God's grace, I met all kinds of people – those who saw the value and those who didn't. In one of my organizations someone said to me – 'how can you be so calm even when someone is yelling at you' and you won't believe I didn't know 'that' about me until then.

I remember thanking that person and telling her in retrospection that, 'I never considered that as a strength, I always thought it was my weakness.' And I still feel that,

maybe it is a strength, but I still need to learn to sharpen the blurry lines between healthy ego and unhealthy ego.

I hope you are not wondering why I keep saying, 'healthy ego' and 'unhealthy ego.' Well, after all these instances, this is one thing I have learnt that 'ego' in itself isn't a bad thing – it's like cholesterol. See the moment we hear the word 'cholesterol' we have an association of it being unhealthy. But our body has LDL and HDL which is bad and good cholesterol respectively.

And the good one is surely helpful to the body. Just like that, the proportion of ego makes it good or bad. You need a healthy amount of ego, so that people don't make a fool out of you, so that you stand your ground for what you feel is right. It's the unhealthy ego that we need to stay away from.

Going back to what I said about me still learning to 'put up my work up there', I hope and believe that you guys will help me with it. I do have few learnings from the first two books I have published but other than that, I am relying on you all to spread the word.

If you have felt, our *meraki* conversations were helpful, drop a DM on my Instagram handle @themerakiwoman.

If you feel these conversations will help other people too, share the book with them.

Basis your feedback, basis all the love and not-so-love that the book receives, I will add or modify in the next edition.

Until then, I will leave you with this final thought by Sadhguru -

Before you expect someone else to be the way you want them to be, you must become the way you yourself want to be.

~ ~ MY MERAKI NOTES ~ ~

www.ingramcontent.com/pod-product-compliance
Lightning Source LLC
LaVergne TN
LVHW050411160726
843469LV00041B/1031

* 9 7 8 9 3 5 6 1 0 6 7 6 5 *